GLASS FUSED ESSENTIALS FOR BEGINNERS

Everything You Need to Know as to Get Started from Step By Step Instruction To Expert Advice

MARC J. PHILIPS

Copyright©2024 Marc J. Philips

All Right Reserved

TABLE OF CONTENT

INTRODUCTION TO GLASS FUSING

1.1 WHAT IS GLASS FUSING?

1.2 THE FASCINATION WITH GLASS

1.3 GETTING STARTED WITH GLASS FUSING

CHAPTER ONE

UNDERSTANDING THE MATERIALS

2.1 TYPES OF GLASS USED IN FUSING

2.2 GLASS COMPATIBILITY

2.3 TOOLS AND EQUIPMENT ESSENTIALS

2.4 SAFETY FIRST: WORKING WITH GLASS

CHAPTER TWO

THE BASICS OF GLASS CUTTING AND PREPARATION

3.1 THE ART OF GLASS CUTTING

3.2 COLDWORKING TECHNIQUES

3.3 PREPARING GLASS FOR FUSING

3.4 USING GLASS FRITS, STRINGERS, AND POWDERS

3.5 ASSEMBLY TECHNIQUES

CHAPTER THREE

FIRING AND KILN OPERATION

4.1 UNDERSTANDING THE FIRING PROCESS

4.2 KILN PROGRAMMING

4.3 ANNEALING: THE KEY TO DURABILITY

4.4 ADVANCED FIRING TECHNIQUES

4.5 Troubleshooting Firing Issues

CHAPTER FOUR

CREATING YOUR FIRST PROJECTS
5.1 Beginner-Friendly Projects

5.2 Designing with Glass

5.3 Working with Molds

5.4 Decorative Techniques

5.5 Customizing Your Pieces

CHAPTER FIVE

INTERMEDIATE AND ADVANCED TECHNIQUES
6.1 Layering and Stacking

6.2 Using Dichroic Glass

6.3 Pattern Bars and Strip Construction

6.4 Pâte de Verre: The Art of Glass Paste

6.5 Advanced Coldworking Techniques

6.6 Incorporating Metal into Glass

CHAPTER SIX

KILN CASTING AND SLUMPING TECHNIQUES
7.1 Introduction to Kiln Casting

7.2 Creating Kiln Cast Pieces

7.3 Slumping Glass into Molds

7.4 Combining Slumping and Fusing

7.5 Casting with Lost Wax Techniques

CHAPTER SEVEN

DISPLAYING AND SELLING YOUR WORK
8.1 Finishing Your Glass Pieces
8.2 Photographing Glass Art
8.3 Selling Your Glass Creations
8.4 Building a Brand as a Glass Artist
8.5 Protecting Your Art: Legal Considerations

CHAPTER EIGHT

MAINTENANCE AND TROUBLESHOOTING
9.1 Caring for Your Kiln
9.2 Glass Fusing Issues and Solutions
9.3 Repairing Broken Glass Pieces
9.4 Storing Glass and Materials
9.5 Long-Term Care of Fused Glass Art

CHAPTER NINE

THE FUTURE OF GLASS FUSING
10.1 Innovations in Glass Fusing
10.2 Sustainable Practices in Glass Fusing
10.3 The Role of Glass Fusing in Contemporary Art
10.4 Inspiration from Master Glass Artists

CHAPTER TEN

RESOURCES FOR GLASS FUSING ARTISTS
11.1 Suppliers and Materials
11.2 Learning and Inspiration
11.3 Glass Fusing Communities and Networks
11.4 Setting Up Your Glass Fusing Studio

CONCLUSION

YOUR JOURNEY WITH GLASS FUSING
REFLECTING ON YOUR GROWTH AS A GLASS ARTIST
STAYING INSPIRED AND MOTIVATED
THE ENDLESS POSSIBILITIES OF GLASS FUSING

APPENDICES

GLOSSARY OF GLASS FUSING TERMS
FIRING SCHEDULES AND TEMPERATURE CHARTS
TROUBLESHOOTING GUIDE
RESOURCES AND FURTHER READING

INTRODUCTION TO GLASS FUSING

Glass fusing, an exquisite form of art that melds creativity with craftsmanship, has been captivating artists and enthusiasts for decades. This introductory section will explore what glass fusing is, delve into its rich history, and reveal both the artistic nuances and the scientific principles that make it a unique craft. Additionally, we will uncover the modern applications and trends that continue to evolve this fascinating art form.

1.1 What is Glass Fusing?

Definition and Overview

Glass fusing involves the process of joining together pieces of glass at high temperatures. Typically, the glass is heated in a kiln at temperatures ranging from 1350 to 1500 degrees Fahrenheit, which causes the pieces to soften and bond together to form a single piece. The result is a fusion of color, light, and texture that can be crafted into countless forms—from jewelry to decorative art to functional objects.

History of Glass Fusing

The roots of glass fusing stretch back to ancient civilizations, with evidence of fused glass artifacts found in Egypt and Rome. Initially, the technique was used to create small decorative items or jewelry. However, it wasn't until the early 20th century that artists began to explore glass fusing as a medium for more substantial art forms. Innovations in kiln technology during the 1970s and 1980s significantly expanded the possibilities for glass fusing, allowing artists to create larger, more complex pieces with greater precision and variety.

The Art and Science Behind Glass Fusing

Glass fusing is as much a scientific process as it is an artistic endeavor. It requires an understanding of the physical properties of glass, including its behavior under heat, its compatibility with different types of glass, and its expansion and contraction. Artists must carefully consider the coefficient of expansion (COE) of the glass to ensure that the pieces being fused will be compatible and will not crack or break during the fusing process.

Modern Applications and Trends

Today, glass fusing has transcended traditional boundaries to include a wide range of applications, from architectural elements like glass tiles and panels to innovative uses in fashion accessories. Technological advancements, such as digital kiln controls and laser cutting tools, have opened new avenues for creativity, precision, and efficiency in glass fusing. Additionally, the growing eco-consciousness has led artists to explore the use of recycled glass, pushing the craft towards more sustainable practices.

1.2 The Fascination with Glass

Why Glass is a Unique Medium

Glass is unparalleled in its ability to transmit, reflect, and refract light, making it a powerful medium for artistic expression. Unlike opaque materials, glass can convey depth and luminosity, creating dynamic interactions with light that change with the viewer's perspective and the surrounding environment.

The Appeal of Creating with Glass

Working with glass offers a sensory experience that is unlike any other art form. The transformation of solid glass into a malleable state and back again provides a magical element to the creative process. For many artists, the allure of glass lies in its dual nature—both fragile and strong, transparent and vibrant.

Glass Fusing vs. Other Glass Art Techniques

While there are several techniques for manipulating glass, including stained glass, glass blowing, and lampworking, glass fusing is unique in its versatility and accessibility. Unlike glass blowing, which requires considerable equipment and skill, glass fusing is more approachable for beginners and can be done in smaller studio spaces with less specialized equipment.

1.3 Getting Started with Glass Fusing

Who Can Try Glass Fusing?

Glass fusing is accessible to anyone with an interest in learning about the craft. It is particularly appealing to those who enjoy experimenting with colors and textures and who appreciate the meticulous details involved in crafting fine art.

Basic Skills Required

The basic skills for starting in glass fusing include cutting glass, understanding kiln cycles, and knowing how to layer glass to achieve different effects. These skills can be developed through classes, workshops, or self-directed practice using various educational resources.

An Overview of the Glass Fusing Process

The glass fusing process involves several key steps: designing your project, cutting and preparing the glass, arranging the glass in the desired design, and firing the assembly in a kiln.

The kiln cycle includes ramping up to fusing temperatures to melt the glass, holding at those temperatures to allow the glass to fuse, and then annealing, which involves slowly cooling the glass to relieve internal stresses. Mastery of these steps allows artists to produce items with both aesthetic beauty and structural integrity.

This introduction provides a foundational understanding of glass fusing, showcasing its historical significance, artistic appeal, and the skills needed to begin exploring this captivating craft. Whether you are drawn to the transformative properties of glass or excited by the prospect of creating art that integrates both beauty and functionality, glass fusing offers a rich and rewarding artistic journey.

CHAPTER ONE
UNDERSTANDING THE MATERIALS
2.1 Types of Glass Used in Fusing

Glass fusing is a captivating art form that involves the transformation of separate glass pieces into a single cohesive item through the process of melting them together inside a kiln. The types of glass selected play a critical role in determining the appearance, functionality, and structural integrity of the final product. Each type of glass offers unique properties and challenges, making understanding these variations essential for both novice and experienced glass artists.

2.1.1 Fusible Glass

Characteristics and Features

Fusible glass is specifically engineered for the purpose of glass fusing. This type of glass is typically available in a wide range of colors and maintains a uniform thickness across different batches, which is essential for consistent fusing results. Its surface is smooth, reducing the need for extensive surface preparation prior to fusing.

One of the defining characteristics of fusible glass is its ability to withstand high temperatures without deforming unexpectedly. The predictability of fusible glass is a crucial aspect for artists who need to plan their projects with precision, as it ensures that the glass will behave in a consistent manner under kiln conditions.

Compatibility Considerations

Not all glass types are suitable for fusing, mainly due to varying rates of expansion and contraction and different melting points. Fusible glass is categorized by its coefficient of expansion (COE), a measure that indicates how much the glass will expand when heated and contract when cooled. Using glass with the same COE is imperative to avoid stress and breakage as the piece cools. Mismatched COE values can lead to cracking or complete breakage of the glass artwork, as different parts of the piece will contract unevenly. It is important for glass fusers to check the COE of all glass pieces used in a project to ensure compatibility.

2.1.2 Sheet Glass
Standard Thicknesses and Colors

Sheet glass is a fundamental material in glass fusing. It typically comes in thicknesses ranging from 1/16 inch (1.6 mm) to 1/4 inch (6 mm), allowing artists to choose the appropriate thickness based on the structural needs and desired optical effects of the project. Sheet glass is also available in an extensive array of colors, from vivid hues to subtle tones, providing a versatile palette for creating a wide range of artistic expressions.

Transparent vs. Opaque

The decision between using transparent and opaque glass impacts the visual dynamics of the fused piece. Transparent glass permits light to pass through, illuminating and enhancing the colors and patterns within the glass, which can add depth and vibrancy to the piece. In contrast, opaque glass blocks light, providing a strong visual presence and rich coloration that can stand out or define areas within the artwork. This makes opaque glass ideal for creating bold

statements and adding contrast.

2.1.3 Accessory Glass
Stringers, Noodles, and Frits

Accessory glass comes in various forms including stringers, noodles, and frits, each adding unique textures and styles to glass fusing projects. Stringers are thin, rod-like pieces of glass that can be used to create delicate lines and details. Noodles are similar but have a flatter and wider shape, making them suitable for bolder lines or borders. Frits are made from crushed glass and are available in different granular sizes from fine to coarse; they are perfect for adding texture, color depth, and intricate patterns to a piece.

Dichroic Glass: Adding Sparkle and Shine

Dichroic glass is a specialty product that has a multi-layer coating of metallic oxides which gives it a unique property of displaying two different colors by reflecting one and transmitting another. This characteristic makes dichroic glass highly desirable for projects that require vibrant, changing colors and a sense of depth. The interplay of light and color can bring dynamic effects to a piece, making it stand out remarkably. It is particularly popular in jewelry and small-scale art pieces where its impact can be fully appreciated up close.

Combining Glass Types

The art of glass fusing often involves combining various types of glass to achieve complex effects and detailed designs. Artists must consider the thermal and physical properties of each glass type, ensuring that all pieces are compatible in terms of COE and that their melting points allow them to fuse properly without causing tension in the finished piece. Advanced techniques may involve layering different types of glass, incorporating stringers or frits into a base of sheet glass, or using dichroic glass to add highlights or focal points.

2.2 Glass Compatibility

Understanding how glass behaves during the heating and cooling processes is crucial for successful glass fusing. The key factor governing this behavior is the Coefficient of Expansion (COE), a measure that can seem abstract but has very tangible effects on the outcome of glass art projects.

Understanding COE (Coefficient of Expansion)

The COE of glass quantifies how much the glass expands when it is heated and contracts when it cools down. This measurement is vital because each type of glass has its unique COE value, and mismatched COE values among different pieces of glass in the same project can lead to stress, cracks, and ultimately, breakage as the glass cools back to room temperature.

Why COE Matters:

- Structural Integrity: Glass with matching COEs will expand and contract at the same rate, maintaining structural integrity throughout the fusing process.
- Predictable Outcomes: Using glass with the same COE makes the behavior of the glass during firing predictable, thus allowing for more accurate design planning.
- Longevity of Art Pieces: Artworks created with compatible glass will be more stable and less prone to damage over time.

It's important to note that the COE is expressed in millionths per degree Celsius ($x10^{-6}/°C$). Common COE values in glass fusing include 90, 96, and 104. Each of these numbers represents a different glass family, and within these families, glass can be mixed with relatively safe results. However, mixing glass from different COE families without special considerations or adjustments typically leads to failure.

How to Match Glass Types for Successful Fusing

Matching glass types by their COE is the first step towards ensuring the compatibility of the materials used in a fusing project. Here's how you can ensure that you use glass with matching COEs effectively:

1. Selecting the Right Glass:

- Consistency: Always purchase glass labeled for fusing, as these typically have well-documented COE values and are made to be used together.
- Supplier Reliability: Buy from reputable suppliers who provide precise and accurate COE values for their glass products.
- Labeling: Keep your glass organized by COE value and clearly label leftovers and scraps to avoid mixing them accidentally in future projects.

2. Mixing Within a COE Family:

- Experimentation: Within the same COE family, feel free to mix colors and textures. This is where the artistry of glass fusing can really shine through, as different glass types within the same COE can still have varying properties when melted.
- Documentation: Keep records of your experiments, including firing temperatures, times, and outcomes. This documentation can help refine future projects and provide a valuable reference.

Testing Glass Compatibility

Even when using glass from the same COE family, variations in color, opacity, and density can affect how each piece behaves under kiln temperatures. Therefore, testing glass compatibility is a critical step before committing to larger, more complex projects.

1. Performing a Compatibility Test:

- Sample Selection: Cut small pieces of each type of glass you plan to use in your project.
- Cleaning: Ensure each piece is clean and free from contaminants that might affect the test outcome.
- Layering: Stack the pieces in the arrangement you plan to use in your final project.
- Firing: Fuse the stack in a kiln, using a standard firing schedule suitable for the glass type.
- Observation: After the piece has cooled, examine it for signs of stress, such as cracks, bubbles, or separation at the interfaces.

2. Analyzing Test Results:

- Compatibility: If the test piece shows no signs of stress or distortion, the glass types used are compatible.
- Adjustments: If any issues are observed, adjustments may be needed either in the firing schedule or in the selection of glass types.
- Documentation: Document the results of each test along with firing conditions to build a comprehensive understanding of how different glass types interact.

Advanced Considerations

For those looking to push the boundaries of glass fusing, understanding the nuanced behaviors of glass beyond COE is crucial. Factors such as glass viscosity at different temperatures and the impact of specific glass colors and chemical compositions on expansion can be explored to create unique effects and textures. Advanced fusers often delve into the science behind glass to manipulate materials in innovative ways, sometimes even using slightly incompatible glass to achieve particular artistic effects under controlled conditions.

Using Incompatible Glass:

- Controlled Incompatibility: In some artistic scenarios, slightly incompatible glass is used deliberately to create specific effects, such as controlled cracking or veining, which can add dramatic effects to the piece.
- Risk Management: This approach requires thorough testing and a deep understanding of glass behavior to avoid complete failure.

2.3 Tools and Equipment Essentials

2.3.1 Kilns

Kilns are the heart of the glass fusing process, providing the necessary environment to heat and melt glass in a controlled manner. The correct selection, use, and maintenance of a kiln are pivotal to achieving desired fusing results.

Types and Sizes of Kilns

Kilns for glass fusing come in a range of sizes and configurations, tailored to different scales of work and studio spaces. The most common types include:

- Tabletop Kilns: Compact and portable, these kilns are ideal for small projects and hobbyists. They typically operate on standard household electrical circuits, making them convenient for use in various settings.
- Studio Kilns: These are larger and designed for medium to large projects, making them a staple in professional studios. They require more power and space but offer greater versatility in terms of the size and quantity of pieces that can be fused at one time.
- Specialty Kilns: These include kilns designed for specific tasks like casting or slumping. They often feature particular elements, such as adjustable shelving or specialized heating elements, to accommodate unique glass fusing techniques.

Choosing the Right Kiln for Your Projects

Selecting a kiln involves several considerations:

- Interior Dimensions: The size of the interior determines how large a piece or how many pieces can be fused at once. It's crucial to choose a kiln that fits the scale of your typical projects.
- Maximum Temperature: Most glass fusing occurs at temperatures ranging from 1300°F to 1500°F. Ensure the kiln can comfortably reach and sustain these temperatures.
- Control Options: Modern kilns come with digital control systems that allow precise temperature control and timing. Programmable controllers enable

artists to set complex fusing cycles with multiple heating and cooling steps.

Kiln Maintenance and Safety

Regular maintenance ensures the longevity and safe operation of your kiln:

- Element Inspection: Check for any signs of wear or damage in the heating elements. Worn elements can affect the temperature accuracy and uniformity.
- Temperature Controller Accuracy: Use a separate pyrometer to verify the kiln's built-in controller. Calibration might be needed to ensure consistent results.
- Cleaning: Remove glass residue and kiln wash after each use to prevent contamination of future projects and to maintain efficient operation.

2.3.2 Cutting Tools

Proper cutting tools are essential for preparing glass pieces before fusing. Each tool plays a specific role in ensuring the glass is appropriately shaped and fits neatly within the design.

Glass Cutters and Scoring Tools

A high-quality glass cutter is indispensable for making precise cuts:

- Wheel Cutters: These are the most commonly used tools, suitable for straight and slightly curved cuts.

The wheel applies a consistent pressure to score the glass.

- Pistol Grip Cutters: Ideal for those who prefer a more ergonomic design, reducing wrist strain during extensive cutting sessions.

Running Pliers and Grozing Pliers

These tools are used after the glass is scored:

- Running Pliers: Designed to apply even pressure along the score line to break the glass cleanly. The curved jaws ensure the pressure is distributed uniformly.
- Grozing Pliers: These are used for nibbling away small pieces of glass to clean up edges or for slight shape corrections.

Grinder: Shaping Your Glass

A grinder is used for smoothing and shaping the edges of cut glass pieces:

- Surface Grinding: Removes sharp edges, making the glass safe to handle and fit better with other pieces.
- Edge Shaping: Allows for precise adjustments in the shape and size of the glass, essential for intricate designs and tight fits.

2.3.3 Molds and Forms

Molds and forms give shape to the glass during the slumping and draping processes that follow the initial fusing. The choice of mold material impacts the quality and characteristics of the final piece.

Types of Molds for Glass Fusing

- Ceramic Molds: These are popular due to their durability and the smooth surface they impart to the glass. They are reusable and can withstand numerous firing cycles.
- Stainless Steel Molds: Offer excellent heat transfer and are particularly useful for projects requiring crisp forms.
- Fiber Molds: Made from refractory fibers, these molds can be custom-shaped and are ideal for one-off designs or prototypes.

Using Ceramic, Steel, and Fiber Molds

Each material offers specific advantages:

- Ceramic: Great for general use, especially for plates, bowls, and other standard shapes.
- Steel: Best for achieving sharp bends and folds in glass, used extensively in architectural elements.
- Fiber: Lightweight and versatile, perfect for artists exploring unique and complex forms.

DIY Molds: Creating Custom Shapes

For artists who frequently need unique shapes or sizes, making your own molds can be a cost-effective and creative solution. Materials like vermiculite board, plaster, and refractory cement are commonly used for DIY mold-making. This approach not only reduces costs but also enhances the artist's control over the final outcome of their projects.

2.4 Safety First: Working with Glass

Safety is of paramount importance when working with glass and operating a kiln. The inherent risks of cutting, shaping, and fusing glass at high temperatures demand a meticulous approach to safety protocols. This comprehensive guide details essential safety gear, best practices for setting up a safe workspace, proper handling techniques for glass, and rigorous fire safety and kiln operation procedures.

Essential Safety Gear

Working with glass, particularly during the fusing process, involves exposure to potential hazards such as sharp edges, hot surfaces, and toxic fumes. It is crucial to equip oneself with the right safety gear to minimize risks:

- Heat-Resistant Gloves: These gloves protect your hands from burns when handling hot glass or kiln shelves. They should be made of materials that can withstand high temperatures without melting or catching fire.
- Safety Goggles: Protecting your eyes is critical when cutting glass or accessing the kiln. Safety goggles should fully cover the area around the eyes, preventing any glass chips, debris, or harmful radiation from causing injury.
- Face Masks or Respirators: When grinding or sanding glass, fine particles can become airborne and pose a respiratory hazard. A face mask or respirator should be used to filter out harmful dust. For those regularly exposed to fine glass particles, a respirator with P100 filters is recommended.
- Protective Clothing: Long sleeves and pants made of natural fibers, such as cotton, help protect the skin

from cuts and burns. Avoid synthetic materials that can melt under high heat.

- Hearing Protection: When using power tools for cutting or grinding glass, protect your hearing with earmuffs or earplugs to prevent long-term hearing damage.

Proper Ventilation and Workspace Setup

Proper ventilation is essential in a glass fusing workspace to safely remove toxic fumes and airborne particles generated during the fusing and cooling process. A well-designed ventilation system ensures a healthy working environment:

- Ventilation System: Install an overhead hood or use local exhaust ventilation at the point of operation to capture fumes directly from the kiln and other sources. This system should be capable of cycling out the air in the room multiple times per hour.
- Workspace Layout: Arrange your workspace to promote clean air flow. Keep the kiln near an exhaust system and ensure that there is no obstruction to air movement. Avoid cramped spaces where fumes can accumulate.
- Regular Air Quality Checks: Use carbon monoxide detectors and regularly check the air quality in your workspace, especially if you use propane or natural gas-fired kilns.

Handling Glass Safely

Handling glass with care is essential to prevent injuries such as cuts or punctures. Following these guidelines can help ensure safe handling practices:

- Cutting Techniques: Always use a professional-grade glass cutter and ensure that the cutting wheel is sharp and oiled. Apply consistent pressure when scoring the glass to create a clean line that requires less force to break.
- Moving and Storing Glass: When moving large sheets of glass, use suction handles or gripping tools to secure the glass firmly. Store glass sheets vertically in a sturdy rack with individual slots to minimize the risk of tipping or breakage.
- Workspace Cleanliness: Keep your workspace free of glass scraps and dust. Regularly sweep and dispose of glass pieces properly. Use a dedicated container for sharp glass waste to prevent accidental cuts.

Fire Safety and Kiln Operation

Operating a kiln safely is critical due to the high temperatures involved and the potential fire hazards:

- Installation and Placement: Ensure that your kiln is installed according to the manufacturer's instructions and local building codes. Place the kiln on a fire-resistant surface and maintain adequate clearance from any combustible materials.
- Regular Maintenance: Inspect your kiln before each use for any signs of wear or damage. Check the integrity of the electrical wiring and elements. Clean the interior of the kiln regularly to prevent the accumulation of kiln wash or glass fragments.
- Fire Safety Equipment: Equip your workspace with a fire extinguisher rated for electrical and general fires. Familiarize yourself with its operation and keep it easily accessible.

- Monitoring Kiln Temperature: Use a reliable pyrometer to monitor the kiln's temperature during operation. Over-firing can lead to overheating and potentially start a fire. Follow the recommended firing schedules and always be present to monitor the kiln during critical heating and cooling phases.

CHAPTER TWO
THE BASICS OF GLASS CUTTING AND PREPARATION

3.1 The Art of Glass Cutting

Glass cutting is a fundamental skill in the world of glass fusing, blending both artistic flair and precise technique to shape glass pieces before they are transformed in the heat of a kiln. This detailed exploration delves into the intricate aspects of glass cutting, covering everything from the basic understanding of glass's unique properties to the mastery of sophisticated cutting techniques necessary for complex and detailed designs.

Understanding Glass Grain and Direction

Unlike many materials used in craft, glass possesses a unique internal structure—it has a 'grain,' akin to the grain found in wood, which significantly influences how it responds to cutting. The grain refers to the directional flow of glass molecules, which impacts its tensile and breaking strength. Recognizing the direction of this grain is crucial; glass tends to break more cleanly and predictably along its grain than against it. This knowledge is invaluable, especially when working with larger or more critical pieces where precision is paramount. Understanding grain direction helps in planning cuts, predicting the glass's behavior under stress, and can be the deciding factor between a successful project and a ruined piece.

Scoring Techniques for Clean Breaks

Scoring is the first step in the glass cutting process, where a small but deliberate scratch is made on the glass surface, using a carbide or diamond-tipped tool. This scratch, or score line, is intended to control the break in the glass, creating a weak spot along which the glass will ideally split when pressure is applied. Achieving a clean break depends significantly on the technique used during scoring. The key factors for successful scoring include maintaining consistent pressure from start to finish and ensuring the motion is smooth and uninterrupted. Too light a score may not sufficiently weaken the glass for breaking, while too heavy a score might cause unwanted cracks or complete shattering.

After the score line is made, tools such as running pliers or breaker-grozier pliers are employed. These tools apply a specific amount of pressure on either side of the scored line, coaxing the glass to break precisely where intended. This stage is delicate, requiring a blend of intuition and experience to perfect.

Advanced Cutting Techniques: Circles, Curves, and Intricate Shapes

Beyond simple straight lines, the world of glass cutting opens up into a realm of complex and dynamic shapes. Circles, curves, and other intricate patterns demand specialized tools and techniques. Tools such as circle cutters provide a perfect solution for cutting precise circular shapes, essential for projects like round window panes or decorative mirrors. These tools pivot around a central point, scoring the glass in a perfect radius.

For more complex curves and intricate designs, band saws and ring saws are the tools of choice. These powerful tools allow for greater creativity, capable of cutting tight curves and intricate details that would be impossible with simpler tools. Band saws use a thin, diamond-coated blade to cut through glass, offering the flexibility to create shapes that are limited only by the artist's imagination. Similarly, ring saws use a circular blade, providing the unique ability to cut in any direction—forward, backward, or sideways—making them ideal for intricate patterns and detailed work in glass art.

These advanced tools require a significant amount of practice and skill to master. The complexity of the cuts they can achieve introduces new challenges, particularly in maintaining the integrity of the glass while maneuvering through tight corners or complex patterns. The precision with which these tools are used can greatly affect the quality and accuracy of the final piece, making skillful cutting an indispensable part of successful glass fusing.

Practical Applications and Creative Exploration

Mastering these cutting techniques opens up a world of possibilities for glass artists. From creating bespoke pieces of art to functional items like bowls, plates, and architectural elements, the ability to cut glass proficiently is key. Each project presents unique challenges and opportunities for creative expression, making glass cutting not just a technical skill but also a form of artistic expression.

Moreover, the process of learning and mastering glass cutting techniques is deeply rewarding. As artists advance their skills, they can experiment with more complex designs and larger-scale projects. The precision and creativity involved in glass cutting make it a continually evolving art form, where each piece reflects both the artist's skill and their artistic vision.

In summary, the art of glass cutting is a critical skill in glass fusing, demanding a deep understanding of the material's properties, mastery over cutting tools and techniques, and an artistic approach to transforming raw glass into intricate designs and functional art. By refining these skills, glass artists not only enhance their ability to execute diverse projects but also elevate their craft to new heights of creativity and precision.

3.2 Coldworking Techniques

Coldworking is an essential process in glass art that involves modifying and refining the glass after it has been cut but before it is fired in the kiln. This process is crucial because it not only enhances the aesthetic quality of the glass but also ensures its safety and functionality. The primary techniques involved in coldworking include grinding and smoothing edges, polishing, and sandblasting, each catering to different aspects of the glass's finish.

Grinding and Smoothing Edges

Once the glass has been cut, it usually has sharp, jagged edges that can be hazardous. The first step in coldworking is to use a glass grinder to smooth these edges. A glass grinder is equipped with a diamond-coated bit that effectively sands down the sharp edges of the glass, making it safer to handle and preventing any damage that could occur from the glass cutting into molds or interfering with other pieces during the fusing process.

The process of grinding not only makes the glass safer but also prepares it for further refinement. For pieces that will fit into a larger composition, it is vital that their edges align perfectly to ensure a seamless integration when fused. This precision can only be achieved through meticulous grinding. Additionally, smoothing the edges helps to prevent defects such as chips and cracks that might develop during the firing process due to uneven stress distributions.

Techniques and Considerations for Effective Grinding

Effective grinding requires steady hands and an eye for detail. Artists must maintain a uniform pressure and use a constant speed to avoid creating grooves or low spots on the glass edges. It's also important to regularly clean and dress the grinder bit to ensure it provides a consistent finish. Water is used extensively during grinding to reduce friction and prevent glass dust from becoming airborne, which could be hazardous to the artist's health.

Polishing Glass for a Finished Look

After the edges of the glass have been sufficiently smoothed, the next step is polishing. Polishing not only enhances the appearance of the glass but also contributes to the tactile quality of the finished piece. For this, cerium oxide, a popular glass-polishing compound, is used along with a felt polishing wheel. The cerium oxide acts as a fine abrasive, smoothing the microscopic roughness left by the grinding process and bringing the glass edges to a glossy finish.

The significance of polishing extends beyond mere aesthetics. In functional pieces such as glassware or tabletops, the smoothness of the edges can significantly impact the user experience. Furthermore, for pieces like jewelry or decorative art, a high polish can enhance the glass's reflective qualities and overall visual impact.

Advanced Polishing Techniques

Advanced polishing techniques may involve multiple stages of polishing compounds, starting with a rougher grit and moving to finer grits for a flawless finish. Sometimes, a cork or pumice wheel is used before the final polish with cerium oxide to prepare the surface better. These additional steps are particularly important for works of art that will be displayed in high-visibility settings, such as galleries or public installations, where every detail counts.

Using a Sandblaster for Surface Texture

Sandblasting is another crucial coldworking technique that offers artists the opportunity to add texture and designs to the glass surface. This technique involves forcefully propelling fine particles, such as aluminum oxide or silicon carbide, against the glass surface. The high velocity of these particles etches away at the glass, creating a frosted appearance or detailed patterns, depending on the artist's design.

Sandblasting is particularly valuable for adding non-slip textures to glassware or functional art pieces. It can also be used to create visual depth and contrast in pieces that combine polished and frosted areas. The ability to control the depth and fineness of the blast allows for a wide range of artistic expression.

Creative Applications of Sandblasting

Artists can use sandblasting to achieve intricate designs by applying a resist or stencil to the glass surface before blasting. The areas covered by the resist remain smooth and clear, while the exposed areas are frosted, creating a stunning contrast. This technique can be used to depict detailed images or patterns, adding a layer of complexity and interest to the piece.

Moreover, sandblasting can be combined with other coldworking techniques to achieve unique effects. For instance, an artist might first etch a design via sandblasting, then polish select areas to create a variety of textures and light reflections within the same piece.

3.3 Preparing Glass for Fusing

The preparation of glass for fusing is a meticulous process that sets the stage for successful art pieces. The cleanliness of the glass, the environment in which it is handled, and the method of arranging and layering each piece all play crucial roles in the outcome of the fused product. This section delves deeper into each of these critical stages to ensure that every glass fusing project begins with the best possible foundation.

Cleaning and Preparing Your Glass

Glass must be impeccably clean before it undergoes the fusing process. Any residue, from fingerprints to fine dust, can prevent the glass pieces from fusing properly or introduce unwanted imperfections into the finished product. The cleaning process involves several steps to ensure that the glass is free of contaminants:

1. Choosing the Right Cleaner: A commercial glass cleaner specifically designed for fusing glass is ideal because it does not leave residues that could affect the fusing process. Alternatively, a mild detergent solution can be used, but it must be thoroughly rinsed off to avoid leaving any film on the glass.

2. Washing Technique: Using lukewarm water, gently wash the glass surfaces with the cleaner using a soft, lint-free cloth or sponge. Avoid using abrasive materials that could scratch the glass.

3. Rinsing: After washing, the glass should be rinsed with clean water to remove any traces of cleaner or detergent. This step is vital to prevent any residues from burning into the glass during fusing, which could alter its clarity and color.

4. Drying: The glass should be dried immediately after rinsing to prevent water spots. A clean, dry, lint-free cloth is ideal for this purpose. Some artists prefer to use a hairdryer on a low heat setting to ensure that the glass is completely dry without introducing dust from a cloth.

5. Final Inspection: Before moving on to the next steps, inspect the glass under good lighting to ensure it is free of fingerprints, streaks, and dust. Any remaining particles can be gently wiped away with a microfiber cloth.

Avoiding Common Contaminants

The fusing process is sensitive not only to the cleanliness of the glass but also to the environment in which it is prepared. Common contaminants can come from various sources:

1. Fingerprints: Oils from the skin can leave prints on the glass that not only affect its appearance but also can create imperfections during fusing. Handling glass with clean cotton gloves after the final cleaning can prevent this issue.

2. Airborne Particles: Dust and other airborne particles can settle on the glass surface even after cleaning. Keeping the workspace meticulously clean and free from dust is crucial. Using air purifiers or maintaining a controlled environment can significantly reduce the amount of airborne debris.

3. Tools and Equipment: Ensure that all tools, from cutters to brushes, are clean before they come into contact with the glass. Contaminants can transfer from dirty tools to the glass surface, embedding unwanted materials into the fused piece.

Layering and Stacking Glass for Desired Effects

Layering glass involves more than just stacking color upon color. It requires an understanding of how different types of glass interact, how they expand and contract, and how they transmit or reflect light. Here are the steps and considerations for effective layering:

1. Understanding COE (Coefficient of Expansion): All glass used in a single project must have a compatible COE to ensure that they expand and contract at the same rate during heating and cooling. This compatibility prevents stress and cracking.

2. Design and Color Planning: Before stacking, plan the design by considering how colors will interact. Lighter colors under darker ones can affect the intensity and hue of the top layers. Using transparent glass over opaque layers can create depth and visual interest.

3. Cutting to Fit: All pieces need to be cut precisely to fit within the planned design. Overlaps should be intentional, not accidental, as they can affect how the glass melts and merges.

4. Stacking Technique: Begin with a base layer and carefully place each subsequent layer on top. Ensure that each piece is aligned according to the design plan. Small pieces of frit or stringer can be used to fill in gaps or add detail.

5. Use of Kiln Paper: Beneath the glass stack, kiln paper can be used to prevent the glass from sticking to the kiln shelf. It also allows for easy removal of the finished piece without damaging the kiln shelf or the glass.

6. Venting: When designing stacked pieces, consider the need for small venting gaps. These allow for air trapped between layers to escape, preventing bubbles and ensuring a smoother surface on the finished piece.

Final Pre-Fusing Checklist

Before placing the glass in the kiln, perform a final check:

- Ensure all layers are clean and aligned.
- Confirm that the kiln shelf is prepared with kiln wash or paper.
- Check the kiln for any residues from previous firings that might affect the current project.

Proper preparation of the glass for fusing is as much an art as it is a science. Each step, from cleaning to stacking, must be carried out with precision to ensure that the final product not only meets the artist's vision but also displays the best qualities of the glass medium. By following these detailed guidelines, glass artists can achieve consistent and satisfying results in their fusing projects.

3.4 Using Glass Frits, Stringers, and Powders

The art of glass fusing is significantly enhanced by the use of accessory materials such as glass frits, stringers, and powders. Each of these materials offers unique properties that allow for the exploration of diverse artistic expressions, from adding intricate details to creating broad, textured surfaces. This section delves deeper into how each of these materials can be used effectively to achieve stunning visual effects in glass fusing projects.

Creating Designs with Frit

Glass frit, which is essentially crushed glass that comes in various granularities from coarse to fine, offers a versatile palette of options for the glass artist. Available in a spectrum of colors, frit can be used to add vibrancy and texture to art pieces. It can be sprinkled or carefully placed to create patterns ranging from abstract randomness to meticulously detailed designs.

Techniques of Working with Frit:

1. Layering for Depth and Texture:

Frit can be layered in between sheets of glass to create multidimensional effects. By altering the amount and colors of frit between layers, artists can achieve a sense of depth that mimics geological formations or abstract landscapes.

2. Creating Gradient Effects:

By gradually changing the color or size of the frit particles from one side of the piece to the other, artists can create beautiful gradient effects. This technique is particularly effective in panels or decorative pieces where a soft transition of color enhances the overall aesthetic.

3. Wet Packing:

This technique involves mixing frit with a binding agent to hold it in place before firing. It allows for precise placement of the frit, making it ideal for detailed designs like floral patterns or intricate borders.

4. Sgraffito:

In this method, layers of different colored frit are laid down, and then parts are scratched away before firing to reveal the colors underneath. This technique is used to create complex, multi-colored images with a textured finish.

Adding Texture and Detail with Stringers and Noodles

Stringers and noodles provide a way to add fine lines and detailed patterns to glass pieces. Stringers are thin, often about the thickness of spaghetti, while noodles are flatter and wider. Both can be clear or colored and are typically made from the same glass used in sheets to ensure compatibility.

Manipulating Stringers and Noodles:

1. Bending and Shaping:

With gentle heat, typically from a candle flame or a small torch, stringers and noodles can be bent into shapes. This flexibility allows artists to create organic shapes like waves, floral stems, or even abstract accents.

2. Combing:

By laying out stringers or noodles parallelly and then running a tool through them while they are slightly heated, artists can "comb" the glass to create wavy or crisscross patterns. This technique is often used in background elements or to add texture beneath a smoother top layer.

3. Inclusion in Cast Glass:

Stringers and noodles can be embedded into clear or translucent cast glass pieces to add interest and complexity. They can form part of a larger picture or serve as minor decorative elements that catch the light differently than the surrounding glass.

Using Glass Powders for Subtle Effects

Glass powders are the finest form of crushed glass and can be used to achieve effects that are not possible with larger glass pieces. They are particularly useful for adding detailed images, subtle color transitions, and even painterly effects to glass art.

Techniques for Using Glass Powders:

1. Painting with Powders:

Mixed with a medium, glass powders can be applied with brushes in a manner similar to painting. This technique allows for the creation of detailed scenes or intricate patterns that are fused into the glass, becoming permanent and vibrant elements of the artwork.

2. Sifting for Soft Backgrounds:

By using sieves of various sizes, powders can be sifted onto the glass surface to create backgrounds or skies in landscapes. The fineness of the powder allows for a soft, almost airbrushed appearance that adds depth without overpowering other design elements.

3. Layering for Shadow and Light:

Glass powders can be layered in different densities to create effects of shadow and light. This technique is particularly effective in creating realistic three-dimensional appearances in fused glass pieces.

4. Creating Texture:

When applied thickly or in multiple layers, glass powders can be used to create textures that mimic natural surfaces like sand, stone, or even rough metal. After firing, these textures can be enhanced by slumping the glass into or over molds to add dimensional form.

By mastering the use of frits, stringers, and powders, glass artists can expand their creative possibilities significantly. Each material offers different properties and challenges, providing a rich toolkit for expressing artistic visions through the medium of glass. These techniques not only enhance the visual appeal of the pieces but also invite tactile interaction, making each piece not just a visual delight but a touchable artifact that holds the imprint of its creator's hands and imagination.

3.5 Assembly Techniques

The assembly of glass for fusing is both an art and a science, involving careful planning, layout, and methodical stacking. This stage is crucial as it directly influences the aesthetic quality and structural integrity of the final piece.

Arranging Glass for Fusing

Proper arrangement of glass pieces on the kiln shelf is essential for successful fusing. The layout must consider not only the design and aesthetic aspects but also the technical requirements of glass fusing, such as heat distribution and glass flow. Each piece of glass expands as it heats and contracts as it cools; thus, spacing is crucial to prevent the glass from sticking to other pieces or the kiln itself.

Key Considerations for Arrangement:

- Spacing: There should be enough space between pieces to allow for expansion but not so much that the pieces become isolated and do not fuse together if so desired.
- Kiln Shelf Preparation: The kiln shelf must be prepared with kiln wash or kiln paper to prevent the glass from sticking to the shelf.

- Gravity: Placement should account for gravity's effect on the glass as it becomes fluid at high temperatures. Strategic placement can help control the direction and flow of the glass.

Techniques for Layering and Creating Depth

Layering multiple pieces of glass is a technique used to add visual depth and complexity to fused glass projects. By carefully stacking different colors and types of glass, artists can create multi-dimensional effects that are not possible with single-layer fusing.

Popular Layering Techniques:

- Pot Melts: In this technique, glass pieces are placed in a ceramic pot with holes in the bottom. As the kiln heats up, the glass melts and drips through the holes onto a prepared shelf below, forming organic and unique patterns.
- Damming: This involves using fiber paper or refractory bricks to contain flowing glass within a designated area on the kiln shelf. It allows for more control over the shape and thickness of the fused piece.
- Inclusions: Adding materials such as copper, silver foil, or compatible ceramics between layers of glass can introduce new colors and effects that enhance the depth and interest of the piece.

Tack Fusing vs. Full Fusing: Deciding on the Right Technique

Choosing between tack fusing and full fusing depends largely on the desired outcome of the project. Each technique offers different characteristics and advantages.

- Tack Fusing: This method involves heating the glass just until it sticks together but retains much of its original texture and form. Tack fusing is ideal for situations where you want to maintain the definition between layers or create a textured surface. The temperature for tack fusing typically ranges between 1250°F and 1350°F (677°C and 732°C).
- Full Fusing: Full fusing is the process of heating glass until it becomes entirely liquid and merges into a uniform piece. This technique is used when a smooth and thoroughly melded piece is desired. The glass is heated to about 1450°F to 1500°F (788°C to 816°C), allowing it to flow together and form a single homogenous layer.

Factors Influencing the Choice Between Tack and Full Fusing:

- Visual Texture: Tack fusing preserves more of the original texture of the glass pieces, while full fusing results in a smooth and glossy surface.
- Structural Integrity: Full fused pieces generally offer greater structural integrity, as the glass layers meld completely.
- Detail Preservation: Tack fusing is preferable when the design requires the preservation of fine details that might otherwise blend together during full fusing.

Final Adjustments Before Fusing

Before the glass is placed in the kiln, it's important to make final adjustments:

- Alignment Check: Ensure all pieces are correctly aligned according to the design plan.
- Cleanliness: Any dust or particles on the glass can result in imperfections; hence, a final cleaning might be necessary.
- Venting: If the design includes enclosed air pockets, small vent holes might be needed to prevent air from expanding and cracking the glass.

CHAPTER THREE
FIRING AND KILN OPERATION
4.1 Understanding the Firing Process
How Glass Behaves During Firing

Glass, in its essence, is an amorphous solid—a material with the structural randomness of a liquid but the mechanical properties of a solid. When glass is subjected to the controlled environment of a kiln, it undergoes a series of transformations dictated by temperature changes, which are crucial not only for achieving the desired artistic outcomes but also for maintaining the integrity and durability of the final piece.

Phases of Glass Transformation in the Kiln

1. Initial Heating: As the kiln's temperature begins to rise, the glass experiences thermal expansion. However, because different parts of a glass piece may heat at different rates— particularly in thicker or more complex pieces—this can lead to stress within the glass. It is during this phase that the risk of thermal shock is highest, which can cause the glass to crack or break if the temperature is increased too rapidly.

2. Softening Point: As the temperature continues to ascend, reaching the glass's softening point, it begins to transform from a rigid state to a more pliable one. This softening allows for the manipulation and shaping of the material. It is at this stage that artists can start to see their individual pieces begin to meld together if multiple pieces are being fused.

3. Full-fuse Stage: Upon reaching the full-fuse temperature, the glass turns fully liquid. In this state, individual pieces of glass flow into one another, eliminating any discernible

boundaries between them, creating a uniform and seamless piece. The exact temperature to achieve this stage varies depending on the type of glass and the desired effect but is generally within the higher range of common fusing temperatures.

4. Annealing Point: Perhaps the most critical stage in the firing cycle, annealing involves cooling the glass to a specific temperature where it can relieve any internal stresses that have built up during the heating process. Maintaining this annealing temperature for an appropriate period is essential to ensure the structural integrity of the glass, allowing it to cool down slowly and evenly thereafter, thus preventing any potential for cracking, breaking, or becoming brittle.

The Importance of Proper Temperature Control

Effective temperature control is vital in glass fusing. It ensures that the glass heats and cools at rates that prevent stress, distortion, or breakage. Utilizing a kiln's thermostat and a reliable pyrometer to gauge the internal temperature accurately is critical. Such precision prevents defects such as devitrification—a process where the glass's surface becomes crystallized, making it appear rough and clouded, thus detracting from its optical clarity and reducing its aesthetic value.

Moreover, proper temperature control helps in achieving consistency in your work, particularly when replicating designs or producing multiple pieces in a series. The ability to precisely control the kiln's atmosphere and the rate of temperature change means that each piece can reach the same level of fusion and clarity, essential for professional-quality glass art.

The Different Phases of Firing: Ramp, Soak, and Cool

1. Ramp: This term refers to the rate at which the kiln temperature increases to reach the desired firing temperature. The ramp rate can have significant effects on the outcome:

- Fast Ramps: Quick temperature increases can lead to thermal shock, which might cause the glass to crack or break. Fast ramps are typically used only when working with small, thin pieces of glass or for specific effects.
- Slow Ramps: More commonly used, slow ramps allow for even heating of the glass, reducing the risk of thermal shock. This is particularly important for thicker or more complex glass assemblies.

2. Soak: During the soak phase, the kiln's temperature is held steady, allowing the entire piece of glass to uniformly reach and hold at the target temperature. This phase is crucial for ensuring thorough fusion or slumping of the glass. The length of the soak will depend on the size and thickness of the glass as well as the desired effect. Longer soaks might be necessary for thicker pieces or for achieving a full-fuse effect.

3. Cool Down: The cooling phase, which includes the critical annealing phase, must be carefully controlled to prevent thermal stress. The annealing phase is tailored specifically to the type of glass and the thickness of the piece, ensuring that the glass cools down at a rate that allows it to stabilize internally:

- Controlled Cooling: Gradually reducing the temperature prevents the formation of stress points that could lead to cracking or breakage.
- Annealing: Proper annealing is essential for ensuring the durability and safety of the glass piece. It involves holding the glass at a specific temperature, known as the annealing point, for a period sufficient to alleviate internal stresses.

The mastery of these firing phases—ramp, soak, and cool—is foundational for any glass artist wishing to explore the realms of glass fusing. Each phase plays a pivotal role in transforming raw glass into a sculpted, artistic creation that is not only beautiful but also structurally sound. Whether creating simple, flat fused panels or more complex 3D sculptures, understanding and controlling the firing process is key to successful glass art.

4.2 Kiln Programming

Setting Up Your Kiln for Different Types of Firing

Programming your kiln correctly is crucial for achieving the desired effects in glass fusing. The correct setup can make the difference between a beautifully fused piece and a disappointing mishap. Kilns can be set for various fusing processes like tack fusing, slumping, or full fusing, each demanding distinct temperature controls and precise timing.

Types of Firing

- Tack Fusing: This process joins glass pieces together without fully melting them, allowing each piece to maintain some individual characteristics. It typically requires lower temperatures and shorter hold times.

- Slumping: Slumping involves heating glass until it becomes soft enough to slump into or over a mold. This technique is perfect for creating bowls, dishes, and other forms.
- Full Fusing: This technique involves heating pieces of glass until they are completely melted together, creating a single homogeneous piece. It requires higher temperatures and longer hold times to ensure all layers meld together smoothly.

Each type of firing serves a specific purpose and requires the kiln to be accurately programmed to achieve the desired artistic effect. Using a programmable kiln facilitates this process, allowing artists to control the heating and cooling cycles with precision.

Understanding Kiln Controllers and How to Program Them

Kiln controllers range from simple manual systems to sophisticated digital controllers. The type of controller significantly impacts the ease and precision of programming the firing schedules.

- Manual Controllers: These are typically operated using switches and dials and require the artist to manually monitor and adjust the temperature throughout the firing process.
- Digital Controllers: These offer more precise control and can store multiple programs for different firing cycles. Digital controllers are highly recommended for complex projects that require specific temperature curves and hold times.

Programming Digital Kiln Controllers

1. Inputting Custom Firing Schedules:

- Step-by-Step Programming: Begin by setting the initial ramp rate, which controls how quickly the kiln reaches the desired temperature. Next, set the target temperature and the hold time for that temperature. Repeat this process for each segment of the firing schedule.
- Layer Considerations: For projects involving multiple layers or types of glass, it's crucial to adjust the ramp rates and hold times to accommodate the differences in thickness and expansion properties.

2. Using Pre-set Programs:

- Many digital controllers come equipped with pre-set programs designed for common glass fusing projects. These programs are based on general best practices and provide a good starting point for beginners.
- Customization: While pre-set programs offer convenience, customizing the programs based on specific project requirements and observations can lead to better results.

3. Monitoring and Adjusting:

- Real-Time Adjustments: During the firing process, it may be necessary to make adjustments based on the behavior of the glass. This could include extending hold times if the glass hasn't fused as expected or adjusting the annealing temperature to prevent stress in the glass.
- Post-Firing Adjustments: After the firing, evaluate the results and adjust future programs accordingly. This iterative process helps refine the firing schedules to better suit specific materials and designs.

Common Firing Schedules and Their Effects

Firing schedules are critical recipes for the heating and cooling of the kiln. They need to be meticulously planned to avoid damaging the glass.

1. Full Fuse Schedule:

- Purpose: To completely melt the glass pieces together.
- Typical Schedule: Fast ramp to 1465°F (800°C), hold for 10 minutes, followed by a controlled cool to annealing temperature.
- Result: A smooth and uniformly fused piece without any discernible layers.

2. Tack Fuse Schedule:

- Purpose: To join glass pieces while retaining their individual textures and appearances.
- Typical Schedule: Fast ramp to 1350°F (730°C), hold for 5 minutes, then cool slowly to prevent thermal shock.
- Result: Pieces are joined but distinctly visible, offering texture and depth to the fused piece.

3. Slump Firing Schedule:

- Purpose: To shape the glass into or over a mold.
- Typical Schedule: Slow ramp to 1250°F (677°C), hold until the glass slumps into the mold, then anneal to relieve stresses.
- Result: Glass takes the shape of the mold, ideal for creating dishes, bowls, and similar forms.

Best Practices for Kiln Programming

- Documentation: Keep detailed records of all firing schedules and the outcomes. This log will be invaluable for troubleshooting and refining processes.
- Test Firing: Always conduct test firings when experimenting with new techniques or materials. This approach minimizes the risk of wasting materials and time on full-scale projects.
- Safety Precautions: Ensure that the kiln is in a well-ventilated area and that all safety protocols are followed to prevent accidents during the firing process.

Effective kiln programming is both an art and a science. It requires understanding the material properties of glass, the capabilities of the kiln, and the desired artistic outcomes. Mastery of this skill opens up endless possibilities in the realm of glass art, allowing for the creation of both functional items and spectacular artistic pieces.

4.3 Annealing: The Key to Durability
What is Annealing and Why is it Important?

Annealing is a controlled process of slowly cooling hot glass after it has been heated in a kiln during fusing or slumping. This crucial step is designed to relieve internal stresses that develop due to temperature gradients within the glass during heating. When glass is heated, its exterior and interior expand at different rates. Without controlled cooling, this disparity can lead to structural weaknesses, making the glass susceptible to cracking, breaking, or even shattering with slight provocations such as changes in temperature or physical shocks.

The importance of annealing cannot be overstated. It converts the glass from a brittle material that could fracture under everyday use into a durable product that can withstand more stress and use. This transition occurs around the annealing point, a specific temperature where the glass is soft enough for molecular movement within the structure, allowing internal stresses to relax.

Proper annealing is vital for both artistic and practical reasons. Aesthetically, it ensures that the glass art retains its desired shape and appearance without distortion. Practically, it enhances the durability and longevity of the glass, ensuring that it remains intact through normal handling and environmental changes.

Annealing Schedules for Different Glass Thicknesses

The annealing process varies significantly depending on the thickness of the glass. Thicker glass retains heat longer, necessitating a slower cooling rate to allow the center and surface to stabilize temperature uniformly:

- Thin Glass (up to 3 mm): This glass cools faster and requires a relatively shorter anneal soak time. However, even with thin glass, rapid cooling can lead to breakage.
- Medium Thickness (4 mm to 6 mm): Most common in glass fusing, this thickness requires a carefully monitored annealing schedule to avoid stress points that could lead to future breakage.
- Thick Glass (over 6 mm): This requires the longest anneal soak times, sometimes extending several hours to ensure that the entire piece reaches thermal equilibrium.

Each type of glass, whether soda-lime, borosilicate, or lead, has its specific annealing temperature, generally at the point where the glass transitions from a brittle state to a plastic state. These temperatures can vary, typically ranging from 900°F to 1100°F (482°C to 593°C), depending on the glass composition.

Avoiding Stress and Cracks Through Proper Annealing

The key to successful annealing is controlling three major factors: the annealing temperature, the anneal soak, and the cooling rate.

- Understanding Annealing Temperatures: It's essential to know the precise annealing point for the type of glass used. This temperature is where the glass is soft enough to allow for internal stress relief without deforming its shape.
- Programming the Anneal Soak: The duration for which the glass is held at the annealing temperature is critical. This soak allows the temperature throughout the thickness of the glass to equalize. The time needed can vary based on the glass's thickness and the complexity of the piece. For example, a simple flat pane will require less time compared to a thick, multilayered sculpture.
- Controlled Cooling: After the anneal soak, the glass must be cooled down to room temperature gradually. The cooling rate should be slow and steady to prevent thermal shock. Programmable kilns can be set to control this rate precisely, but even manual kilns can be managed effectively with careful monitoring.

Advanced Techniques in Annealing

For artists working with complex shapes or large fused pieces, advanced annealing techniques may be required:

- Segmented Annealing: This involves using multiple hold points during cooling to address particularly thick or unevenly distributed areas of glass.
- Stress Testing: In some cases, especially for functional items like glass tableware, stress tests using polarized light can help identify and rectify residual stresses before the piece is completed.
- Computerized Kiln Controls: Modern kilns equipped with sophisticated computerized controls can automatically adjust the heating and cooling rates based on the specific requirements of the glass piece being annealed.

Common Challenges and Solutions in Annealing

- Cracks and Breakage: These are often the result of too rapid cooling. Adjusting the cooling rate and ensuring a uniform temperature across the piece can mitigate these issues.
- Devitrification (Cloudy Glass): This can occur if the glass spends too much time at high temperatures. Reducing soak times or adjusting the peak temperature can help maintain clarity.
- Compatibility Issues: Using glass pieces from different manufacturers or lines can lead to stress due to different expansion coefficients. Testing for compatibility before fusing large pieces is crucial.

4.4 Advanced Firing Techniques
Tack Fusing vs. Full Fusing: What's the Difference?

1. Tack Fusing:

Tack fusing is a delicate process where glass pieces are heated until they just begin to stick together but are not fully fused into one smooth sheet. This technique allows the individual pieces to retain much of their original texture and form, making it ideal for projects where the visual distinction between components is desirable. Artists often use tack fusing to add dimension and depth to their works, creating layered effects that enhance the overall aesthetic appeal. The key to successful tack fusing lies in precise temperature control; the kiln must reach just enough heat to start the fusing process without fully melting the glass, typically around 1350°F to 1400°F.

During tack fusing, each piece of glass softens slightly and adheres to its neighbors, but distinct boundaries remain visible. The result is a textured surface where each piece can be distinctly felt and seen, often used for artistic pieces like mosaics or complex geometric designs. It's essential to monitor the kiln closely during this process to ensure that the glass does not overheat, which could cause the pieces to fully blend together, defeating the purpose of tack fusing.

2. Full Fusing:

In contrast, full fusing involves heating pieces of glass to a point where they completely melt together, forming a uniform and smooth piece without any demarcations between the original glass pieces. This technique requires higher temperatures, usually between 1450°F and 1500°F. Full fusing is commonly used when a sleek, smooth finish is desired, such as in making glass sheets for further cutting or creating a canvas for painting and printing.

The full fuse cycle allows the glass to reach a stage where it becomes fluid and flows together, filling any gaps and smoothing out any irregularities. The pieces meld into a single entity, losing their individual edges to create a solid, durable piece. Full fusing is particularly beneficial for functional items like dishes or panels where a smooth surface is critical for both aesthetic and practical purposes.

3. Comparative Considerations:

Choosing between tack fusing and full fusing depends largely on the desired outcome of the project. Tack fusing preserves more of the glass's original character and texture, while full fusing offers a more uniform and polished end product. Artists may select one technique over the other based on the visual effect they aim to achieve or the specific functional requirements of the finished piece.

Slumping: Shaping Glass into Forms

Slumping is another transformative technique in glass fusing that involves heating a glass sheet just enough so it becomes malleable and slumps into or over a mold. Typically performed at temperatures around 1200°F to 1350°F, slumping does not melt the glass fully but softens it so it can adapt to a new shape under the influence of gravity.

This technique is often used to create bowls, plates, and other three-dimensional objects. The choice of mold is crucial in slumping, as it determines the form the glass will take. Molds can be made from various materials, including ceramic, stainless steel, or specially formulated refractory materials designed to withstand high temperatures without cracking or warping.

1. Practical Applications:

Slumping is particularly popular for making functional art pieces like dishes and light fixtures, which benefit from the gentle contours and shapes that can be achieved with this technique. Artists can also slump glass into more abstract forms, allowing for creative expression in sculptures and decorative art pieces.

2. Considerations and Tips:

When slumping glass, it's important to prepare the mold with a release agent to prevent the glass from sticking. Monitoring the kiln temperature and duration is crucial to achieving the desired slumping without over-softening the glass, which can cause it to distort or lose detail.

Fire Polishing: Achieving a Glossy Surface Finish

Fire polishing is a finishing technique used to refine and smooth the surface of glass after it has been fused and shaped. By reheating the glass to just below the full fuse temperature, typically between 1300°F and 1350°F, the surface of the glass reaches a point where it just starts to melt, causing any minor imperfections or roughness to "heal" and form a glossy finish.

1. Applications of Fire Polishing:

This technique is particularly useful for pieces where a shiny, flawless surface is essential, such as in jewelry, tabletops, or decorative art where every detail matters. Fire polishing can also be employed to smooth the edges of a piece, reducing sharpness for safer handling and a more polished appearance.

2. Technique and Control:

The key to effective fire polishing lies in the control of the heating process. The glass must be heated quickly to the target temperature, held briefly, and then cooled down slowly to prevent stress and cracking. This rapid heating causes only the surface to melt, preserving the integrity of the shape and details of the glass piece.

Fire polishing can transform a piece from a craft project to a professional-grade work of art, enhancing its transparency, brightness, and overall visual impact. It is an indispensable technique for any glass artist looking to elevate the quality of their work.

By mastering these advanced firing techniques—tack fusing, full fusing, slumping, and fire polishing—glass artists can significantly expand their creative repertoire and improve the quality of their finished projects. Each method offers unique possibilities and can be tailored to specific artistic visions, making them fundamental skills for any serious practitioner of glass fusing.

4.5 Troubleshooting Firing Issues

Glass fusing is both an art and a precise science, requiring an understanding of materials, processes, and equipment. Despite careful planning and execution, artisans can encounter several common problems during the firing process. Addressing these issues effectively not only saves pieces from being discarded but also enhances the skill set of the glass artist.

Common Problems and Their Solutions

1. Bubbles in Glass

Bubbles are one of the most frequent issues in glass fusing. They can occur for several reasons, such as trapped air between layers of glass, moisture in the kiln, or overly rapid heating. To manage and minimize bubbles:

- Slow Ramp: Increase the heating rate slowly to allow air trapped between layers to escape before the glass becomes too viscous.
- Venting: Allow the kiln to vent during the early stages of firing (up to 500-600 degrees Celsius) to enable moisture and air to escape.
- Bubble Squeeze: Incorporate a bubble squeeze segment in your firing schedule. This involves holding the temperature at a point where the glass is soft enough to allow air to escape but not so fluid that it traps more air.

2. Cracks in Glass

Cracks can result from thermal shock, incompatible glass COE (coefficient of expansion), or uneven heating. To prevent cracks:

- Compatible Glass: Always use glass with compatible expansion coefficients to ensure even expansion and contraction during heating and cooling.
- Gradual Temperature Changes: Avoid sudden temperature changes in your firing schedule. Ensure that the kiln heats and cools gradually to reduce stress on the glass.
- Proper Annealing: Invest time in properly annealing your glass, especially thick pieces, to relieve internal stresses.

3. Devitrification

Devitrification is the process where the glass surface becomes crystallized and cloudy during firing. This can detract from the clarity and brilliance of the piece. To avoid devitrification:

- Clean Glass Thoroughly: Before placing your glass in the kiln, ensure it is clean and free from contaminants like oils and fingerprints, which can seed crystalline growth.
- Use Devitrification Spray: There are commercial sprays available that help to prevent devitrification by forming a barrier on the glass surface.
- Optimal Firing Temperatures: Firing at too high a temperature or holding at high temperatures for too long can encourage devitrification. Adjust your firing schedules to avoid excessive peak temperatures.

Understanding Kiln Behavior and Adjusting Accordingly

Each kiln has its unique quirks, such as uneven heating elements, insulation differences, and general wear and tear, which can affect firing results. To understand and adapt to your kiln's behavior:

- Monitor Firing: Use witness cones or small test pieces in different parts of the kiln to monitor how uniformly the kiln is heating.
- Kiln Surveys: Conduct a kiln survey to identify hot and cold spots. This can be done by placing a series of pyrometric cones throughout the kiln and observing their response after a standard firing cycle.
- Regular Maintenance: Keep the kiln in good repair. Regularly check elements, thermocouples, and relays for signs of wear or failure, which can impact temperature accuracy and uniformity.

Recovering from Firing Mishaps: Cracks, Bubbles, and More

Despite the best preparation, firing mishaps can still occur. Knowing how to salvage a project is a valuable skill in glass fusing. Here are some techniques for repairing common issues:

1. Grinding Away Imperfections

When bubbles or devitrification mar the surface of a piece, it can often be ground away. Using a glass grinder:

- Remove the Top Layer: Carefully grind away the affected area until you reach clear glass.
- Polish: After grinding, the surface will be rough; it needs to be polished back to its original shine, which can be done through fire polishing or using cerium oxide.

2. Filling Cracks

Cracks can sometimes be repaired by filling with frit (small granules of glass) or by inserting thin strands of compatible glass into the crack and refiring the piece. This method:

- Clean the Crack: Ensure the crack is clean and free from debris.
- Apply Adhesive: Use a glass adhesive to hold the frit or glass strands in place during the initial phase of refiring.
- Refire: Carefully ramp up the temperature to allow the filling material to fuse without stressing the glass further.

Adding a Layer of Clear Glass

For pieces severely affected by devitrification or coarse surface textures, covering the piece with a layer of clear glass and refiring can encapsulate imperfections, giving it a fresh, glossy surface. This approach:

- Prepare the Surface: Clean the original piece thoroughly.
- Cut Clear Glass: Cut a piece of clear glass to the exact size of the original piece and lay it on top.
- Fire Again: Refire at a temperature just high enough to fuse the clear layer to the base without fully melting the details underneath.

By mastering these troubleshooting techniques, glass artists can ensure that their work is not only beautiful but also structurally sound, minimizing loss and maximizing the artistic expression of their glass fusing endeavors.

CHAPTER FOUR
CREATING YOUR FIRST PROJECTS
5.1 Beginner-Friendly Projects
Simple Coasters: A Perfect First Project

Creating your first set of glass coasters is an excellent way to become familiar with the essentials of glass cutting, arranging, and fusing. Begin by selecting small, evenly sized pieces of fusible glass. Choose clear or colored glass based on your preference and the design intent. Standard shapes like squares and circles are great for starting out. These basic forms allow you to focus on achieving uniform thickness and smooth edges, which are crucial for even fusing.

Experiment with adding a pop of color by including small pieces of compatible glass. Compatibility is key; ensure all glass pieces have the same coefficient of expansion (COE) to prevent stress fractures during the firing process. You can introduce simple geometric patterns or even abstract designs by arranging smaller glass bits in creative ways on the base piece. This project not only aids in understanding the fusing process but also how different pieces bond when exposed to high temperatures. It's a practical introduction to glass art, providing a foundational experience in handling and designing with glass.

Creating a Fused Glass Pendant

A pendant offers a small, manageable canvas to explore more detailed designs, making it an ideal project for beginners wanting to delve a bit deeper into the craft of glass fusing. Start with a base piece of glass, typically a small rectangle or circle. Layer smaller elements on top to create depth and intricate details. You might include bits of dichroic glass, which are known for their sparkling, metallic appearance, adding a vibrant or iridescent quality to your pendant.

Incorporate thin strands of glass called stringers, which can be laid out in patterns or gently bent to create organic shapes. When layering these elements, it's crucial to maintain the same COE across all types of glass used to ensure the piece fuses evenly and avoids any stress fractures during firing. This project is an excellent way to experiment with light, color, and transparency on a small scale, providing valuable lessons in glass behavior and the aesthetic potential of different materials.

Making Decorative Tiles

Decorative tiles offer a canvas for more expansive artistic expression and are an excellent way to experiment with various inclusions and textural effects. Begin with a larger base of clear or colored glass that will serve as the backdrop for your design. On this base, you can experiment with adding different types of inclusions such as frit (crushed glass), confetti (thin shards of glass), and small glass rods. These elements can be sprinkled or arranged in specific patterns to create visual interest and texture.

Tiles provide a flat surface that is perfect for exploring different decorative techniques like stencil designs or silk-screening with glass powders. Silk-screening, in particular, allows for the application of intricate graphic designs that can be fused into the glass surface. You might also consider experimenting with reactive glass that changes color based on the heat and the specific elements it interacts with during the firing process.

This project is a wonderful opportunity to learn how heat transforms various textures and shapes of glass. As the glass melts and fuses, unique patterns and effects emerge, each influenced by the arrangement and type of glass used. The decorative tile project not only enhances your understanding of material behavior under high temperatures but also expands your ability to create aesthetically pleasing designs with glass.

Project Completion and Learning

Completing these beginner-friendly projects provides foundational skills and confidence in glass fusing. Each project builds upon the last, gradually increasing in complexity and introducing more techniques and materials. As you progress from making simple coasters to more complex pendants and decorative tiles, you'll gain a deeper appreciation for the craft and understand the various factors that influence the final outcome, such as glass compatibility, heat control, and creative design.

These initial projects serve not only as practice pieces but also as stepping stones to more advanced glass fusing work. They encourage creativity and experimentation while providing a practical understanding of the glass fusing process. As you become more comfortable with these projects, you'll be well-prepared to tackle larger and more complex works, equipped with the knowledge and skills needed to create beautiful, functional, and decorative glass art.

5.2 Designing with Glass
Choosing Colors and Patterns

The selection of colors and patterns in glass fusing is not only about aesthetic appeal but also about how the colors interact and transform under high temperatures. Understanding color theory can play a pivotal role here.

Complementary colors—colors opposite each other on the color wheel, like blue and orange or red and green—can create vibrant contrasts that stand out strikingly in a piece. Analogous colors, which are next to each other on the color wheel, offer a more harmonious and serene visual experience, blending smoothly from one shade to the next.

When designing with glass, consider the opacity and transparency of each piece. Transparent glass allows light to pass through and colors to layer, which can create deep, multidimensional visual effects. Opaque glass offers a solid, rich color that can be used to create bold statements and strong visual lines. Additionally, the texture of the glass—smooth, rough, or bubbled—can affect how it interacts with light, adding another layer to the complexity of your design.

Using different patterns can enhance your projects as well. Geometric patterns, stripes, and polka dots can be used for a modern look, while softer lines and curves may lend a more organic feel to the piece. Techniques such as stringer application, where thin strings of glass are laid down to create patterns, or using frit (crushed glass) to fill in shapes, can add detail and texture to your work.

Using Negative Space and Layers

Negative space in glass design is the area where the glass isn't, and this space can be as impactful as the areas filled with glass. By arranging glass pieces to create gaps, you allow light to play through these spaces, bending and reflecting in intriguing ways. This technique can highlight certain aspects of your design and give the illusion of depth and movement.

Layering is another crucial technique in glass fusing. By carefully planning the arrangement of different layers of glass, you can control the flow and interaction of the glass as it heats and melts together. This can create stunning visual effects, such as depth or the appearance of floating elements within the glass. However, it's essential to balance the layers to ensure they enhance rather than overwhelm the overall design. This might involve using thinner layers of glass or varying the sizes and shapes of the pieces you are working with to maintain a coherent visual weight across the piece.

Incorporating Found Objects and Mixed Media

Integrating non-glass materials into your glass projects can bring an unexpected texture and character to your work. Common materials include metals, ceramics, and even sand. However, it's crucial to ensure that any material included can withstand the fusing temperatures, which often exceed 1400 degrees Fahrenheit.

Metals, for example, can add a reflective quality or act as a resist, creating negative spaces where the glass doesn't flow. When using metals such as copper or silver, they can react with the glass to create stunning, colorful halos due to the chemical interaction at high temperatures. Ceramics can be used similarly, though they typically do not melt into the glass and instead provide a texture contrast.

Sand can be used to create texture or as part of a mold, where glass fuses around and over it, leaving a gritty, textured impression in the glass once the sand is removed after firing. Another approach is incorporating organic materials, such as leaves or fibers, which will burn away during firing, leaving their impressions or voids in the glass, offering a subtle yet captivating inclusion that adds to the narrative of the piece.

When using mixed media, consider the thermal compatibility and the coefficient of expansion (COE) of the materials. This ensures that the glass and the inclusions expand and contract at a similar rate, reducing the risk of stress fractures or breakage during the cooling process.

Each material introduces its own set of challenges and possibilities, and testing is often required to understand how these materials interact with glass. Experimentation is key in discovering unique combinations that withstand the fusing process while enhancing the aesthetic and structural integrity of your creations.

5.3 Working with Molds
Selecting the Right Mold for Your Project

Choosing the right mold for your glass fusing project is crucial and can significantly influence the final outcome. The most common materials for molds include ceramic, silicone, and metal, each with distinct advantages and considerations:

- Ceramic Molds: These are popular for their ability to withstand high temperatures and their versatility in shape and size. Ceramic molds are excellent for detailed designs as they hold their shape well under the heat. When selecting a ceramic mold, consider the complexity of the design and ensure that the mold's contours can accommodate the glass expansion and contraction during the firing process.
- Silicone Molds: Known for their flexibility and non-stick properties, silicone molds are a great choice for beginners. They are easier to handle and release from the glass than ceramic molds, making them ideal for intricate shapes and sizes. Silicone also allows for easy cleaning and storage, but it may not offer the same level of detail as ceramic or the durability of metal.

- Metal Molds: These molds are durable and excellent for repeated use, making them a preferred choice for production work where the same shape is required multiple times. Metal molds heat up and cool down quickly, which can affect the glass fusing process. It's important to monitor the firing schedule closely when using metal molds to prevent the glass from cooling too quickly, which can lead to thermal shock.

When selecting a mold, consider the final shape you wish to achieve. Each material interacts differently with heat, and understanding these interactions helps in achieving the desired results while avoiding issues like sticking or uneven fusing.

Preparing Molds with Kiln Wash or Mold Release

Before you begin your glass fusing project, preparing the mold is a step that cannot be overlooked. Applying a kiln wash or mold release agent is essential to ensure that the glass does not adhere to the mold during the firing process. Here are detailed steps and considerations:

- Application of Kiln Wash: Kiln wash is a mixture of silica and kaolin clay that acts as a separator between the glass and the mold. It should be applied in thin, even layers. Start by mixing the kiln wash according to the manufacturer's instructions, then use a haik brush to apply it smoothly over the mold's surface. Allow the kiln wash to dry completely, which can take several hours depending on the ambient temperature and humidity.
- Using Mold Release Agents: In some cases, especially with intricate molds, a standard kiln wash might not be sufficient. In such scenarios, a mold release spray

or a liquid form release agent can be used. These agents often provide a stronger barrier and are easier to apply in even coats. They are particularly useful for silicone and metal molds where fine details might be lost with thicker layers of kiln wash.

Regular maintenance of the mold's coating is crucial. After each use, inspect the layer of kiln wash or mold release for any cracks, flaking, or thinning areas. Reapply as necessary to ensure that the glass does not stick to the mold during subsequent firings, which can ruin both the mold and the glass piece.

Shaping Glass: Plates, Bowls, and Vessels

Creating functional items like plates, bowls, and vessels starts with choosing a suitable mold and preparing it with kiln wash or mold release. The process of shaping glass using molds is both an art and a science:

- Setting Up the Glass: Begin with cutting the glass to the approximate size and shape of the mold. Clean the glass thoroughly to remove any fingerprints or debris that could burn into the surface during firing. Arrange the glass pieces on the mold. For bowls or deeper vessels, consider using a dam or fiber paper around the edges to maintain the glass's shape during the slumping phase.
- Firing the Glass: The glass must be heated slowly to the slumping or fusing temperature, which will depend on the glass type and thickness. As the glass heats, it becomes soft and begins to conform to the shape of the mold. Watching this process can provide valuable insights into how glass moves and reacts to heat.

- Cooling and Finishing: Once the glass has shaped into the mold, it must be cooled or annealed properly. Improper cooling can lead to stress fractures or warping. After the piece has cooled, remove it from the mold and inspect it for any rough edges or imperfections, which can be smoothed using grinders or coldworking techniques.

5.4 Decorative Techniques
Adding Details with Enamel and Glass Paints

Enamels and glass paints are integral to adding vibrant colors and intricate details to glass art pieces, offering a palette that can transform the aesthetic of any work. The process begins with selecting the right type of enamel or paint—options vary from opaque to transparent, each creating a different visual effect when fused. When using enamels, artists have the option of either sifting the powder onto the glass or mixing it with a medium to paint it on. This method is particularly useful for creating precise designs or adding fine details like small characters or intricate patterns.

The application of glass paints and enamels can be done in multiple layers, with each layer requiring a firing cycle. This layering technique not only intensifies the color depth but also adds a dimensional quality to the glass. It's essential to monitor the firing temperatures closely—too high, and the paint may burn off or bubble; too low, and it might not fuse properly, resulting in a weak bond that could peel or flake over time. Typically, firing temperatures for enamels range from 1,300 to 1,500 degrees Fahrenheit, depending on the specific product and desired effect.

Another exciting aspect of using enamels and glass paints is the ability to create reactive effects. Certain colors contain metals that react with each other when heated, creating unique, unpredictable patterns and hues. This unpredictability can be a boon for artists looking to create one-of-a-kind pieces, as the interaction between layers of different colors can yield truly stunning results.

Using Inclusions for a Unique Look

Inclusions offer a distinctive way to add interest and texture to glass pieces. This technique involves embedding objects within the glass layers that either remain intact or burn away during firing. Common inclusions are metals such as copper, silver leaf, or screen meshes, which can add a shimmering effect or create interesting visual textures. Organic materials like leaves, paper, or even thin fabrics can also be used; these materials burn away in the kiln, leaving behind a ghostly imprint or ash, enclosed within the glass, which can evoke a sense of mystery and depth.

The key to successful inclusions is understanding how different materials react under intense heat. For instance, some metals may oxidize and change color, adding an unexpected twist to the design. It's also crucial to consider the compatibility of the glass with the inclusion material to prevent stress fractures or disintegration during the cooling phase. Properly calculating the annealing curve—where the glass is allowed to cool slowly to relieve internal stresses—is critical, especially when working with thick or heavily layered pieces.

Creating Textures with Embossing Techniques

Embossing glass is a tactile technique that involves manipulating the glass surface when it's in a semi-molten state, usually during the initial phases of firing. By using various tools—such as stamps, molds, or even simple utensils—artists can press patterns directly into the surface of the glass, creating raised or indented areas. This technique not only adds visual depth but also a physical texture that can dramatically alter the glass's light-catching properties.

One popular method of embossing involves laying a stencil over the glass and then sprinkling frit (crushed glass) around it. When the glass is fired, the areas under the stencil lack the frit layer, creating a beautiful contrast in both texture and color. Alternatively, artists can use fiber paper cutouts placed between layers of glass; as the glass fuses, it flows around the fiber paper, which burns out, leaving a raised pattern.

Embossing can be further enhanced by combining it with other decorative techniques, such as painting or adding inclusions. For example, after embossing a pattern into a piece, an artist might add a wash of enamel over the raised areas to accentuate the texture or apply a thin sheet of silver leaf to add a reflective quality. These combined techniques can create complex, multi-dimensional effects that make each piece a unique work of art.

Integrating Multiple Techniques for Complex Designs

The beauty of glass fusing lies in the ability to integrate multiple decorative techniques to create sophisticated, intricate designs. For instance, an artist might start with a base layer of glass painted with enamels. They could then add inclusions such as copper wires or dichroic glass pieces for sparkle and texture. Once the initial elements are in place, embossing could be used to introduce physical depth to the design before a final layer of clear glass is added to encapsulate all the elements together.

As artists gain experience, they often begin to experiment with these techniques, pushing the boundaries of what can be achieved with glass. This exploration can lead to unique stylistic signatures that make their work instantly recognizable. Whether through the subtle hues of layered enamels, the dramatic flair of metallic inclusions, or the tactile appeal of embossed textures, glass artists use these techniques not just to beautify but to tell stories and evoke emotions, making each piece a narrative as much as it is an object of art.

5.5 Customizing Your Pieces

Personalization with Decals and Transfers

Personalization is a key aspect of glass fusing that allows artists to add a unique touch to their creations. Decals and transfer papers are crucial tools in this process. They enable the application of detailed graphics, intricate patterns, or text onto glass surfaces. These designs are first printed onto special transfer papers using ceramic or glass paints. Once the design is prepared, the paper is positioned on the glass surface and the piece is taken to the kiln.

During the firing process, the decal material fuses seamlessly into the glass, permanently embedding the design within the piece. This method is particularly effective for creating personalized gifts, decorative home items, or custom pieces with company logos or artistic designs. The precision of this technique allows for high-detail imagery that can range from fine text to complex multicolored patterns, making each piece distinct and tailored to specific tastes or branding requirements.

Adding Lettering and Images to Your Glass

For those looking to incorporate text or detailed imagery directly onto the glass, sandblasting and etching are the preferred techniques. Sandblasting involves using a high-pressure jet of fine sand directed at the glass surface through a stencil. This abrasive action selectively wears away the surface of the glass where the stencil exposes it, creating a frosted, matte finish that can beautifully contrast with the untouched, glossy areas of the glass.

Etching, on the other hand, uses a chemical process to achieve a similar frosted effect. An acid-resistant resist is applied to the glass in the pattern or design of your choice, and acid is then applied to etch the exposed areas. Both techniques are excellent for adding decorative lettering, logos, or intricate designs that require precise detail and texture contrast on the glass surface. These methods can transform ordinary glass pieces into elegant artworks or functional items with enhanced aesthetic appeal.

Exploring Surface Treatments: Etching, Sandblasting, and More

While etching and sandblasting are popular, there are other surface treatment techniques that can add depth and intrigue to glass art. One such technique involves using reactive glass paints. These paints contain special ingredients that undergo a chemical reaction when heated in the kiln, changing color and creating vibrant, multi-tonal effects on the glass. This can result in stunning visual effects that are not achievable through traditional colored glasses or enamels.

Another advanced technique is the application of luster overcoats. Lusters are metallic compounds that, when applied to glass and fired, produce a shimmering metallic sheen or iridescent finish. This can add a luxurious feel to any piece, making it stand out as a centerpiece or a decorative accent. The sheen achieved with lusters can vary from a subtle pearlescence to a bold, mirror-like finish, depending on the composition of the luster and the firing conditions.

Artists may also explore layering these techniques to create complex, multi-dimensional surface designs. For example, one might first etch a pattern into the glass, then apply reactive paint within the etched areas to highlight the design with a burst of color once fired. Subsequently, a luster might be added for an elegant finish. The possibilities are virtually limitless, and each combination of techniques can open up new avenues for artistic expression.

Combining Techniques for Custom Creations

The true beauty of glass fusing lies in the ability to combine these various customization techniques to produce pieces that are not only visually striking but also deeply personal. Whether it's through the subtle nuances of etched glass, the boldness of decals, or the intricate details achievable with sandblasting, each technique offers its own set of creative challenges and rewards.

By experimenting with different surface treatments and personalization methods, artists can continually push the boundaries of what is possible in glass fusing. The result is a diverse portfolio of works that not only showcases the versatility of glass as a medium but also reflects the personal artistic journey of the glass fuser. This ongoing exploration of techniques and styles not only enhances the aesthetic value of the pieces created but also deepens the artist's connection to their craft, making each project a meaningful and fulfilling endeavor.

CHAPTER FIVE
INTERMEDIATE AND ADVANCED TECHNIQUES

6.1 Layering and Stacking

Creating Multi-Layered Projects

Layering and stacking are foundational techniques in glass fusing that allow artists to add complexity and visual interest to their work. The concept is simple: by placing multiple layers of glass on top of one another, you can create designs that have depth, richness, and a unique interaction of colors. However, achieving the desired effects requires an understanding of the properties of different types of glass, as well as the technical nuances of the fusing process.

When you begin experimenting with layering, it's essential to consider the types of glass you are working with. Glass comes in a variety of transparencies and colors, each affecting how light interacts with the finished piece. For instance, transparent glass allows light to pass through, illuminating the layers beneath and creating a sense of depth and dimensionality. On the other hand, opaque glass blocks light, providing a solid background that can make the colors and textures of the upper layers stand out more vividly.

In your initial projects, start with simple designs such as coasters or small dishes. These manageable projects allow you to observe how different colors and transparencies interact during the fusing process. For example, placing a layer of clear glass over a patterned opaque glass can magnify the pattern and add a subtle sheen. Conversely, layering multiple colors of transparent glass can result in new, blended hues that change depending on the angle of the light.

As you gain confidence, you can begin experimenting with more complex projects that involve multiple layers of different colors and types of glass. Strategic layering can create intricate designs where different colors and patterns emerge, shift, or blend as the viewer's perspective changes. This dynamic quality is one of the most compelling aspects of working with layered glass, offering endless possibilities for artistic expression.

Achieving Depth with Transparent and Opaque Glass

Achieving a sense of depth in your glass pieces involves a thoughtful combination of transparent and opaque glass. Each type of glass plays a distinct role in the overall aesthetic of the piece, and understanding how to balance these elements is key to mastering the layering and stacking technique.

Transparent glass is invaluable for creating a sense of lightness and depth in your work. When used in combination with opaque glass, it can highlight or obscure underlying layers, depending on how it is positioned. For example, placing a transparent layer over a bright, opaque color can soften the color's intensity, giving the piece a more nuanced, ethereal appearance. Similarly, transparent glass can be used to create "windows" within a piece, where the underlying colors and patterns are partially visible, drawing the viewer's eye deeper into the composition.

Opaque glass, on the other hand, acts as a solid foundation. It can be used to anchor the design, providing contrast that makes the transparent layers above it more striking. Opaque glass is particularly effective when you want to highlight a specific area of your design or when you want to create bold, graphic elements that stand out sharply against the more delicate, translucent layers.

One technique to explore is alternating layers of transparent and opaque glass to create a sense of depth and movement. For instance, you might place an opaque layer at the bottom, followed by a transparent layer, another opaque layer, and so on. This approach can create a visually complex piece where the interaction of light and color shifts depending on the viewer's perspective and the light source.

Experimenting with patterns in your layering is another way to add depth. For example, cutting transparent glass into shapes or strips and layering them over an opaque background can create intricate designs that appear to float above the surface. The interaction between light, color, and shadow in these pieces can be mesmerizing, making the artwork appear almost three-dimensional.

Controlling the Flow of Glass

Controlling how glass flows during the fusing process is crucial to preserving the integrity of your design, especially when working with multiple layers. As glass is heated in the kiln, it begins to soften and flow. If not carefully managed, this flow can cause the layers to merge in unintended ways, potentially distorting your design.

One of the key factors in controlling the flow of glass is understanding how different types of glass behave at high temperatures. For instance, glass with a higher viscosity will flow less than glass with a lower viscosity. This means that the type and thickness of glass you use in each layer will affect how much movement occurs during the fusing process.

Another important technique for controlling flow is the use of damming. Damming involves creating a barrier around the edges of your piece to contain the glass as it flows and expands during the firing process. This can be done using fiber paper, refractory bricks, or specially designed kiln dams. By preventing the glass from spreading too much, you can maintain clean edges and sharp details in your design.

For intricate layered pieces, it's also essential to consider the firing schedule. A slow ramp-up in temperature allows the glass to fuse gradually, reducing the risk of excessive flow. Similarly, holding the kiln at specific temperatures for longer periods can help ensure that each layer fuses at the right rate, maintaining the distinctiveness of each layer.

Advanced techniques include using controlled bubbles within the layers to create texture and depth. By trapping small air pockets between layers of glass, you can create a piece that has a subtle, organic feel. These bubbles can be controlled by adjusting the spacing between the layers, the temperature of the kiln, and the rate at which the glass is heated.

6.2 Using Dichroic Glass
What is Dichroic Glass?

Dichroic glass is a fascinating material that has captivated artists and scientists alike since its inception. The term "dichroic" comes from the Greek words "di," meaning two, and "chroma," meaning color. True to its name, dichroic glass can display two different colors depending on the angle of view and the light source. This unique characteristic is achieved through a complex manufacturing process involving a vacuum deposition technique, where multiple layers of metal oxides (such as titanium, silicon, and magnesium) are applied to the surface of glass in a vacuum chamber.

Originally developed for the aerospace industry, dichroic glass was designed to serve as an optical coating that could reflect infrared light while allowing visible light to pass through. This technology was crucial in applications like satellite mirrors and spacecraft windows, where controlling heat and light was essential. However, the glass's striking visual properties soon caught the attention of the art world, leading to its adoption in various creative disciplines, including glass fusing, jewelry making, and sculpture.

In glass fusing, dichroic glass is highly prized for its ability to create stunning, iridescent effects. The multiple layers of metal oxides create a shimmering, metallic sheen that changes color as the viewer's perspective shifts. This ability to reflect one color while transmitting another gives dichroic glass a magical, otherworldly quality that adds depth and dimension to any glass project. Artists often use dichroic glass to create focal points or to add a touch of brilliance to their work, making it a favorite material for both decorative and functional art pieces.

Techniques for Incorporating Dichroic Glass into Your Work

Incorporating dichroic glass into your glass fusing projects requires a thoughtful and precise approach due to its unique properties and relatively high cost. To make the most of this material, it's essential to start with a clear vision of how you want to use it in your design. Given its high impact and cost, dichroic glass is often used sparingly, as small accents or focal points, within a larger piece made of more economical base glass.

When working with dichroic glass, cutting it into smaller pieces allows you to maximize its effect while minimizing waste. These smaller pieces can be strategically placed within your design to draw the viewer's eye and create a sense of movement or focus. For example, in a piece of fused glass jewelry, a small fragment of dichroic glass can serve as the centerpiece, surrounded by more subdued materials to highlight its brilliance.

It's also important to consider the orientation of the dichroic coating during the cutting and assembly stages. Dichroic glass comes in two main varieties: coated on one side, known as "single-sided," and coated on both sides, known as "double-sided." Depending on your design, you may choose to place the coated side facing up to maximize its reflective properties, or you may want to sandwich the dichroic layer between other layers of glass to achieve a more subtle effect.

One of the challenges of working with dichroic glass is its sensitivity to heat. The dichroic coating can change color or even lose its reflective properties if the glass is fired at too high a temperature or for too long. To avoid these issues, it's crucial to conduct test firings with small samples of dichroic glass to determine the optimal firing schedule for your kiln and project. These tests will help you understand how the dichroic glass behaves under different conditions and allow you to adjust your technique accordingly.

In some cases, you may want to experiment with layering dichroic glass with other types of glass to create complex, multi-dimensional effects. For example, placing a layer of clear or lightly tinted glass over a piece of dichroic glass can enhance its reflectivity and create a sense of depth. Conversely, placing dichroic glass under a layer of translucent glass can soften its appearance and integrate it more seamlessly into the overall design.

Creating Eye-Catching Effects with Dichroic Glass

Dichroic glass's ability to interact with light makes it an ideal material for creating eye-catching effects in your glass fusing projects. Its iridescence and color-shifting properties can transform a simple piece into a dazzling work of art, capturing and reflecting light in ways that are both dynamic and captivating.

One of the most popular uses of dichroic glass is in jewelry making. Small pieces of dichroic glass can be fused into pendants, earrings, or rings, where their shimmering colors add a touch of elegance and luxury. Because jewelry pieces are often viewed up close, the intricate details and color variations of dichroic glass are particularly effective in this medium. When designing jewelry, consider how the piece will move and catch the light, as this will enhance the visual impact of the dichroic glass.

In addition to jewelry, dichroic glass can be used in larger fused glass projects, such as wall panels, sculptures, or even functional items like bowls and plates. In these cases, dichroic glass can be used to create focal points within the design, drawing the viewer's attention and adding a sense of movement and life to the piece. For example, a wall panel might feature a central motif made from dichroic glass, surrounded by more neutral colors and textures to emphasize the brilliance of the dichroic element.

When creating layered or stacked glass pieces, dichroic glass can be placed between layers of clear or lightly tinted glass to amplify its reflective qualities. This technique not only enhances the visual depth of the piece but also protects the dichroic coating during firing. The result is a piece that seems to glow from within, with colors that shift and change as the viewer moves around it.

For more experimental projects, consider using dichroic glass in combination with other materials, such as metal inclusions or textured surfaces. The contrast between the smooth, reflective surface of the dichroic glass and the rough, tactile quality of metal or textured glass can create a striking visual effect. Additionally, using dichroic glass in sculptural forms, where light can penetrate and reflect off multiple surfaces, can lead to unexpected and beautiful results.

6.3 Pattern Bars and Strip Construction
Making Pattern Bars for Unique Designs

Pattern bars are a fascinating technique in glass fusing that allow you to create intricate, repeating designs within a single piece of glass. The process begins with the careful selection of different colors of glass, which are then stacked in a mold. The choice of colors is crucial, as the way these colors interact during the heating process can dramatically alter the final appearance of the pattern bar. The magic of pattern bars lies in the way colors blend and flow together when heated, creating unexpected and often mesmerizing results.

To create a pattern bar, you typically start with base layers of glass, which can be clear, opaque, or a combination of both. These layers are then built up with additional pieces of colored glass, each cut and placed with precision. The stacking order and the thickness of each layer are important factors that influence the final design. For example, placing thin strips of color between thicker layers of clear glass can create a subtle gradient effect, while alternating opaque and transparent layers can add depth and complexity to the pattern.

After the glass is stacked in the mold, it is placed in the kiln and subjected to a full fuse cycle. During this process, the glass melts and flows together, creating a solid block of fused glass. The temperature and duration of the firing process are critical, as too much heat can cause the colors to overblend, while too little can result in incomplete fusion. Once the firing is complete, the glass is allowed to cool slowly in a controlled manner, a process known as annealing, to prevent thermal shock and ensure the glass is strong and stable.

Once the fused block is cool, it is carefully removed from the mold and sliced into cross-sections. These slices reveal the intricate patterns created by the layered glass, each one a unique work of art. The slicing process requires precision and the use of specialized tools, such as a diamond saw, to ensure clean, even cuts. The resulting pattern bars can be thin or thick, depending on the intended use, and each slice can be further refined through coldworking techniques like grinding and polishing.

The versatility of pattern bars is one of their greatest strengths. The slices can be used as design elements in a wide range of projects, from jewelry to large architectural panels. Because each slice is a cross-section of the original stack, it carries with it a piece of the entire design, making it possible to create a series of related pieces that share a common visual theme. Pattern bars can also be combined with other glass fusing techniques, such as tack fusing or slumping, to add even more dimension and interest to your work.

Strip Construction: Creating Bold, Geometric Patterns

Strip construction is another powerful technique for creating bold, geometric designs in glass. Unlike pattern bars, which are created by stacking glass, strip construction involves cutting strips of glass and arranging them side by side on a kiln shelf. The strips can be of varying widths and colors, allowing for endless possibilities in terms of design.

The process begins with cutting the glass into strips using a glass cutter and straightedge. The strips can be uniform in width for a clean, orderly appearance, or varied for a more dynamic, irregular design. When cutting the strips, it's important to consider how the colors will interact when fused together. For example, placing a dark strip next to a light one can create a striking contrast, while placing complementary colors next to each other can produce a more harmonious effect.

Once the strips are cut, they are carefully arranged on the kiln shelf in the desired pattern. The alignment and spacing of the strips are crucial for achieving a clean, uniform appearance after fusing. Even slight misalignments can become more pronounced after the glass is fused, so it's important to take your time during this stage. You can use a ruler or guide to help maintain consistent spacing between the strips, or experiment with different arrangements to create more organic, flowing patterns.

After the strips are arranged, the glass is placed in the kiln and fired to a full fuse. During the firing process, the strips melt and fuse together, forming a single, cohesive piece of glass. The resulting fused piece can then be used as-is, or it can be further manipulated through additional firing cycles, such as slumping, to add shape and dimension.

Strip construction is particularly well-suited for creating modern, abstract designs that emphasize clean lines and bold colors. The technique lends itself to a wide range of applications, from small decorative objects like coasters and tiles to larger, more complex pieces like wall panels and architectural installations. The simplicity of the technique belies the potential for complexity and sophistication in the final design, making it a favorite among both beginners and experienced glass artists.

Using Pattern Bars and Strip Construction in Fused Glass Projects

Once you have created your pattern bars or strip construction pieces, the possibilities for incorporating them into larger projects are virtually limitless. Pattern bars, with their intricate, repeating designs, can be used as focal points in a variety of projects. For example, you might slice a pattern bar into thin strips and use them as decorative accents on a larger panel, or you might use a single slice as the centerpiece of a pendant or brooch.

Pattern bars can also be used in combination with other glass fusing techniques to create more complex, multi-layered pieces. For example, you could layer a slice of pattern bar with other pieces of glass and fuse them together to create a piece with both depth and texture. Alternatively, you could incorporate pattern bars into a slumped piece, adding dimension and shape to the design.

Strip construction pieces, with their bold, geometric patterns, are equally versatile. They can be used on their own to create striking, modern designs, or they can be combined with other techniques to add complexity and interest. For example, you might create a strip construction panel and then add a layer of frit or stringer for additional texture. Or you might slump a strip construction piece into a bowl or dish, creating a functional piece of art.

Both pattern bars and strip construction offer a unique way to explore color, pattern, and form in glass. By experimenting with different combinations and techniques, you can create pieces that are not only beautiful but also uniquely your own. Whether you're creating a simple tile or an elaborate wall panel, these techniques provide a foundation for endless creativity and innovation in the art of glass fusing.

6.4 Pâte de Verre: The Art of Glass Paste
Introduction to Pâte de Verre Techniques

Pâte de Verre, a term derived from French meaning "paste of glass," represents one of the most exquisite and intricate techniques in the art of glassmaking. Unlike other glass-forming methods, Pâte de Verre involves the meticulous process of mixing finely crushed glass, often referred to as frit, with a binding agent to create a malleable paste. This paste is then carefully applied to the interior surface of a mold, layer by layer, allowing the artist to build up color, texture, and detail with remarkable precision.

The origins of Pâte de Verre date back to ancient Egypt, where it was used to create small decorative objects. However, it gained prominence in the late 19th and early 20th centuries, particularly through the work of French glass artists such as Henri Cros and Albert Dammouse, who revived and refined the technique. Today, Pâte de Verre is celebrated for its ability to produce delicate, translucent, and highly detailed glass pieces that are often seen as the pinnacle of glass art.

One of the defining characteristics of Pâte de Verre is the control it offers over the glass's final appearance. By varying the size of the glass particles and the composition of the binder, artists can achieve a wide range of effects, from smooth, polished surfaces to rough, textured finishes. Additionally, because the glass paste can be applied in very thin layers, Pâte de Verre allows for the creation of intricate designs and patterns that would be challenging, if not impossible, to achieve using other glass-forming techniques.

Creating Delicate, Detailed Glass Pieces

The true beauty of Pâte de Verre lies in its ability to produce glass art that is not only visually stunning but also rich in texture and detail. This technique is particularly well-suited for creating pieces with complex designs, such as floral motifs, intricate patterns, or even sculptural forms. The process begins with the careful preparation of the mold, which is typically made of plaster, silica, or a refractory material that can withstand the high temperatures of the kiln.

Once the mold is prepared, the artist mixes the glass frit with a binder, usually a liquid such as gum arabic or a cellulose-based material. The consistency of the paste can be adjusted depending on the desired effect, with thicker pastes allowing for more texture and thinner pastes providing a smoother finish. The artist then applies the paste to the mold using a variety of tools, such as brushes, spatulas, or even their fingers, to build up the design layer by layer.

One of the key advantages of Pâte de Verre is the ability to control the color and opacity of the final piece. By layering different colors of glass frit, the artist can create subtle gradients, vivid contrasts, or intricate patterns that add depth and complexity to the work. Additionally, the translucency of the glass allows light to pass through the layers, creating a luminous, almost ethereal quality that is unique to this technique.

The artist's ability to manipulate the paste also extends to the creation of textures and surface finishes. For example, by varying the size of the glass particles, the artist can achieve a range of textures, from fine, sand-like surfaces to coarse, pebbled finishes. This versatility makes Pâte de Verre an ideal technique for artists who want to experiment with different surface treatments and explore the tactile qualities of glass.

Firing and Finishing Pâte de Verre Projects

Firing is the most critical stage in the Pâte de Verre process, as it determines the final appearance and structural integrity of the piece. Because the glass paste is applied in thin layers, it is essential to fire the piece at the correct temperature to ensure that the layers fuse together without distorting the intricate details. Typically, the kiln is heated slowly to allow the glass to reach its fusing point without causing thermal shock, which can lead to cracking or warping.

The firing process for Pâte de Verre is often divided into multiple stages, each with its own specific temperature and duration. The first stage, known as the burnout or dehydration phase, involves gradually heating the piece to around 150-200°C (300-400°F) to remove any moisture from the binder. This step is crucial to prevent the formation of bubbles or other imperfections during the subsequent stages of firing.

Once the dehydration phase is complete, the kiln temperature is gradually increased to the fusing point, typically between 700-800°C (1300-1500°F), depending on the type of glass and the desired effect. During this phase, the glass particles soften and fuse together, creating a solid, unified structure. Careful monitoring of the kiln temperature is essential to avoid over-firing, which can cause the glass to slump or lose its shape, particularly in delicate, detailed areas.

After the fusing stage, the piece is slowly cooled, a process known as annealing, to relieve internal stresses that can lead to cracking. The annealing process involves holding the piece at a specific temperature, usually around 500°C (930°F), for several hours before gradually cooling it to room temperature. This step ensures that the glass cools evenly, reducing the risk of thermal shock and ensuring the durability of the final piece.

Once the firing is complete, the piece is removed from the kiln and carefully demolded. At this stage, the artist can begin the finishing process, which may involve additional coldworking techniques to refine the edges, smooth the surfaces, and enhance the overall appearance of the piece. Coldworking can include grinding, polishing, sandblasting, or acid etching, depending on the desired finish.

6.5 Advanced Coldworking Techniques

Coldworking is an essential skill for any glass artist who wants to elevate their work from good to exceptional. It refers to the processes used to shape, refine, and finish glass after it has been fused or cast, often adding the final touches that give a piece its polished, professional appearance. Advanced coldworking techniques can transform your glass projects by allowing you to achieve precision in shaping, high-gloss finishes, and the integration of intricate designs. Let's delve into these advanced techniques and how they can enhance your glass fusing projects.

Using Laps and Diamond Tools for Precision Shaping

Precision shaping is a cornerstone of advanced coldworking. The tools most commonly used for this are laps, grinders, and diamond tools, each serving a distinct purpose in the coldworking process. Laps, which are flat, rotating discs coated with abrasive materials, are particularly useful for creating flat surfaces, straight edges, and precise angles. They come in various grit sizes, allowing you to progress from rough shaping to fine polishing. When using a lap, it is crucial to maintain a steady hand and consistent pressure to achieve uniform results. The quality of your work on the lap can greatly influence the final appearance of your glass piece.

Diamond tools, including diamond saws and grinders, offer unmatched precision and versatility in shaping glass. These tools can cut, grind, and smooth glass surfaces with exceptional accuracy, making them indispensable for creating complex shapes and detailed features. For instance, a diamond grinder can be used to carve intricate curves, bevel edges, or even create delicate inlays in a fused glass piece. The key to successful use of diamond tools lies in understanding the different grits and how they affect the glass surface. Coarse grits remove material quickly but leave a rough finish, while finer grits are used for smoothing and polishing.

One advanced technique involves using a combination of laps and diamond tools to create beveled edges on glass. Beveling not only adds a decorative element but also enhances the structural integrity of the glass. This process involves first grinding the glass to the desired angle using a coarse diamond grinder, then refining the edge with progressively finer laps until the bevel is smooth and polished. The result is a clean, sharp edge that reflects light beautifully, adding depth and sophistication to your work.

Creating High-Gloss Finishes

A high-gloss finish is often the final step that transforms a piece of glass from ordinary to extraordinary. Achieving a flawless, mirror-like surface requires a combination of skill, patience, and the right tools. One of the most common methods to achieve a high-gloss finish is fire polishing. This technique involves placing the finished glass piece back into the kiln and heating it just enough to allow the surface to melt slightly, creating a smooth, glossy finish. Fire polishing can be tricky, as overheating the glass can cause it to slump or lose its shape. Therefore, it's important to closely monitor the kiln temperature and carefully control the firing schedule.

Another method to achieve a high-gloss finish is mechanical polishing using compounds like cerium oxide. Cerium oxide is a fine abrasive powder that, when mixed with water to form a slurry, can be applied to the glass surface using a felt pad or a polishing wheel. The slurry works to gradually remove microscopic scratches and imperfections, resulting in a smooth, shiny surface. Mechanical polishing with cerium oxide is particularly effective for flat surfaces and edges, making it ideal for finishing projects such as fused glass tiles, coasters, or panels.

For more intricate or curved surfaces, a combination of hand polishing and mechanical tools may be necessary. Start with a medium-grit diamond pad to remove any major scratches or irregularities, then switch to a fine-grit pad for smoother results. Finally, use cerium oxide to achieve that high-gloss finish. The key to successful polishing is consistency; each stage of the process should be thorough, with all previous marks removed before moving on to the next step. Rushing through the polishing stages can result in a less-than-perfect finish, so patience is essential.

Incorporating Coldworking into Complex Designs

Coldworking is not just a finishing step; it's a powerful tool for adding complexity and depth to your glass designs. Techniques like etching, carving, and engraving allow you to create intricate patterns and textures that are impossible to achieve through fusing alone. These methods involve removing material from the glass surface to create designs, often with the aid of specialized tools like diamond burrs, sandblasters, or engraving pens.

Etching is one of the simplest and most versatile coldworking techniques. It involves using a resist (such as vinyl tape or a stencil) to protect parts of the glass surface while the exposed areas are sandblasted or acid-etched to create a frosted appearance. This technique can be used to add subtle patterns, lettering, or images to the glass, providing a unique texture that contrasts with the smooth, glossy areas.

Carving and engraving are more advanced techniques that allow for deeper, more detailed designs. Carving involves using diamond tools to remove larger amounts of glass, creating three-dimensional effects or deep grooves in the surface. Engraving, on the other hand, is typically used for more delicate, fine-line work, such as intricate patterns or detailed imagery. These techniques can be combined with other coldworking processes, like polishing, to create multi-dimensional designs that play with light and shadow, adding depth and complexity to your work.

One advanced application of these techniques is to create layered designs, where different layers of glass are coldworked individually before being fused together. This method allows for the creation of intricate, multi-layered pieces with designs that appear to float within the glass. For example, you could engrave a design on a layer of clear glass, fuse it with a layer of colored glass, and then coldwork the surface to reveal parts of the design in different colors. The result is a piece with a rich, layered appearance that showcases the depth and beauty of glass.

Incorporating coldworking into your glass projects opens up a world of creative possibilities. Whether you're adding subtle details or creating bold, intricate designs, these advanced techniques allow you to push the boundaries of what's possible with glass. By mastering the use of laps, diamond tools, and polishing compounds, you can achieve professional-quality finishes that elevate your work to new heights. And by exploring the artistic potential of etching, carving, and engraving, you can create glass pieces that are not only beautiful but also uniquely your own.

6.6 Incorporating Metal into Glass
Techniques for Adding Metal Elements

Incorporating metal into glass fusing projects introduces a fascinating layer of complexity and creativity. Metals can interact with glass in unique ways, creating effects that are impossible to achieve with glass alone. Adding metal elements allows you to play with contrasts—combining the organic, sometimes unpredictable nature of metal with the smooth, polished finish of fused glass.

One of the most common techniques involves the use of copper foil. Copper, with its relatively low melting point and interesting reactions with glass, is a favorite among glass artists. Copper foil can be cut into intricate shapes and designs, then sandwiched between layers of glass. During the firing process, the copper oxidizes, often resulting in a rich, reddish-brown hue that contrasts beautifully with the surrounding glass.

Wire inclusions are another popular technique. Thin wires, typically made of copper, silver, or nichrome (a nickel-chromium alloy), can be embedded in glass to create linear patterns or structural elements. These wires retain their form and shine, even after firing, providing a striking contrast to the smooth surface of the glass. Wire can be used to outline shapes, add texture, or create a framework within the glass piece.

Sheet metal offers a more substantial way to incorporate metal into glass art. Thin sheets of metal can be cut, shaped, and layered between glass sheets. As the glass melts and fuses in the kiln, the metal can shift slightly, creating organic, fluid shapes within the glass. The edges of the metal may oxidize, adding an additional layer of color and texture to your piece. These sheets can be left to fully encapsulate the glass or partially exposed for a more textured finish.

Beyond these standard techniques, artists are increasingly experimenting with more unconventional methods. Metal powders and flakes, for example, can be sprinkled between layers of glass to create a speckled or marbled effect. Additionally, some artists incorporate metal leaf (extremely thin sheets of metal) to add a subtle shimmer and reflective quality to their work. Each of these techniques requires careful consideration of the properties of both the glass and the metal, as their different thermal expansions and reactions to heat can lead to unexpected results.

Creating Metal Inclusions: Copper, Silver, and Gold

Metal inclusions are an advanced technique that involves embedding metals directly into the glass before it is fired in the kiln. Copper, silver, and gold are the most commonly used metals for this purpose, each bringing its own unique characteristics and challenges.

Copper, for example, is a versatile metal that can produce a wide range of effects depending on how it is used. When copper is heated in the kiln, it can oxidize, change color, or even create a patina that adds depth and richness to the glass piece. Copper wire, foil, or thin sheets can be placed between layers of glass, and as the glass fuses, the copper can create delicate lines, shapes, or even abstract patterns. The interaction between the copper and the glass can result in anything from a bright, shiny finish to a deep, earthy tone, depending on the temperature and firing conditions.

Silver, while more expensive, offers a different set of possibilities. Silver inclusions can produce a bright, reflective quality that stands out against the glass. When silver is heated in the kiln, it can also undergo a process called reduction, where the oxygen is removed from the metal, leading to a metallic finish that contrasts sharply with the surrounding glass. Silver wire can be twisted or shaped into intricate designs, while silver leaf can add a luxurious touch to the surface of the glass. The key to working with silver is to understand its behavior under different firing conditions, as it can easily be overwhelmed by the glass if not handled correctly.

Gold, often used in leaf or foil form, adds an element of opulence to glass art. Gold is more stable under high temperatures compared to copper and silver, retaining its luster and color through the firing process. However, its high cost means it is often used sparingly, as an accent or focal point within a piece. The inclusion of gold can create a striking contrast with darker glass colors, or it can be used to highlight specific areas of a design. Gold leaf, in particular, is often applied to the surface of the glass after firing and then fired again at a lower temperature to bond it to the glass, resulting in a rich, metallic finish that elevates the entire piece.

Combining Glass and Metal for Unique Artistic Effects

The combination of glass and metal opens up a world of artistic possibilities, allowing you to create pieces that are not only visually striking but also structurally innovative. Metals can be used to reinforce the glass, create new textures, or even introduce new colors through chemical reactions during the firing process.

One of the most exciting aspects of combining glass and metal is the potential for creating mixed-media art. Metal meshes, rods, or recycled metal objects can be embedded in the glass, creating a blend of textures and materials that challenges the traditional boundaries of glass art. For example, incorporating a metal mesh within a glass panel can create a grid-like pattern that adds depth and structure to the piece. Alternatively, using metal rods as a framework can allow for the creation of more sculptural, three-dimensional forms.

Recycled metal parts, such as old keys, gears, or even scrap metal, can also be used to add a sense of history or narrative to your work. These elements can be fused within the glass, partially exposed, or used to create texture on the surface of the glass. The contrast between the aged, industrial metal and the smooth, glossy glass can create a powerful visual impact, making your work stand out as both contemporary and timeless.

Experimentation is key when working with glass and metal. By varying the placement of the metal, adjusting the firing temperature, or combining different metals within a single piece, you can achieve a wide range of effects. It's important to document your experiments and results, as the interaction between glass and metal can be unpredictable. Over time, you will develop a deeper understanding of how these materials work together, allowing you to push the boundaries of your artistic expression.

Each of these techniques requires practice and patience to master fully. As you delve into the world of incorporating metal into glass, you'll find that the possibilities are endless. Whether you're aiming for subtle inclusions that add a hint of color and texture, or bold, structural elements that redefine the shape and form of your glass, working with metal will expand your creative horizons and deepen your appreciation for the intricate dance between these two materials.

CHAPTER SIX
KILN CASTING AND SLUMPING TECHNIQUES

7.1 Introduction to Kiln Casting

What is Kiln Casting?

Kiln casting is a specialized glass-forming technique where glass is melted and shaped inside a kiln using molds. Unlike other glass fusing methods, kiln casting allows for the creation of three-dimensional objects with intricate details. This technique involves placing glass pieces or powders into a mold and then heating them until the glass melts and takes on the shape of the mold. Once the glass has cooled and solidified, the mold is removed to reveal the cast glass object. Kiln casting is often used to create sculptures, decorative items, and functional art pieces.

Kiln casting offers several advantages, including the ability to create complex shapes that would be difficult or impossible to achieve through other glass-forming methods. It also allows for the precise control of color, texture, and surface finish, making it a popular choice for artists and designers looking to create unique and detailed glassworks.

Materials and Tools for Kiln Casting

To successfully execute kiln casting, you will need specific materials and tools. The primary material is glass, which can be in the form of frit (small pieces of glass), chunks, or sheet glass cut into shapes. The type of glass you use should be compatible with kiln casting, with a focus on ensuring that the glass has a consistent coefficient of expansion (COE) to prevent cracking or distortion during the firing process.

The tools required for kiln casting include:

- Kiln: The most important tool, as it is used to heat the glass to its melting point. The kiln must be capable of reaching and maintaining the high temperatures required for kiln casting.
- Molds: Molds are essential for shaping the glass. They can be made from various materials, including plaster, ceramic, or metal, and are designed to withstand the high temperatures of the kiln.
- Kiln Wash or Mold Release: These materials are applied to the mold to prevent the glass from sticking to it during the casting process.
- Glass Cutting Tools: If you are using sheet glass, you will need tools to cut and shape the glass before placing it in the mold.
- Measuring and Mixing Tools: These are used to measure and mix materials for making molds, particularly if you are creating custom molds for your casting project.
- Protective Gear: Safety is paramount when working with glass and high temperatures. You will need heat-resistant gloves, safety goggles, and proper ventilation in your workspace.

Creating Molds for Kiln Casting

Molds are the foundation of kiln casting, and creating them requires careful planning and precision. The mold is what gives the glass its final shape, so the quality and detail of the mold directly impact the finished piece. There are several methods for creating molds, each with its own set of techniques and materials.

1. Plaster and Silica Molds:

Plaster and silica molds are among the most common for kiln casting. The process begins with creating a model of the desired object, which can be made from clay, wax, or another material. This model is then used to form a negative mold by pouring a mixture of plaster and silica over it. Once the plaster has hardened, the model is removed, leaving behind a cavity in the shape of the object. This cavity will be filled with glass during the kiln casting process.

These molds are known for their ability to capture fine details, making them ideal for intricate designs. However, they are generally single-use, as they are broken to remove the cast glass piece after firing.

2. Ceramic Molds:

Ceramic molds are durable and can be reused multiple times. They are made by pressing clay into or around a model and then firing the clay to harden it. The resulting mold is sturdy and can withstand repeated exposure to the high temperatures of the kiln.

These molds are often used for larger or more complex projects where reusability is an advantage. Ceramic molds are also excellent for slumping, where the glass is draped over the mold and allowed to conform to its shape during firing.

3. Silicone Molds:

Silicone molds are flexible and can be used to create detailed, intricate designs. However, they are not suitable for direct exposure to the kiln's high temperatures. Instead, silicone molds are often used to create wax or other soft material positives, which are then used to make plaster or ceramic molds.

This method is particularly useful for creating complex, multi-part molds or when working with delicate designs that require a high level of detail.

4. Lost Wax Molds:

The lost wax technique involves creating a detailed model in wax, which is then encased in a mold material such as plaster. Once the mold has hardened, the wax is melted and drained away, leaving a cavity that can be filled with glass. This method is ideal for creating highly detailed, one-of-a-kind pieces.

The choice of mold material and technique depends on the specific requirements of your project, including the level of detail, size, and whether you need a reusable mold.

7.2 Creating Kiln Cast Pieces
Preparing the Mold: Tips and Techniques

The success of a kiln casting project hinges on the proper preparation of the mold. Before placing any glass into the mold, it is crucial to ensure that the mold is clean, free of debris, and properly coated with kiln wash or mold release. This coating prevents the glass from sticking to the mold, making it easier to remove the finished piece without damaging it.

1. Applying Kiln Wash:

Kiln wash is a protective coating applied to the interior surfaces of the mold. It acts as a barrier between the glass and the mold, preventing them from fusing together. To apply kiln wash, mix the powder with water according to the manufacturer's instructions and brush it onto the mold in a thin, even layer. Allow it to dry completely before placing glass in the mold.

2. Mold Release Sprays:

In some cases, especially with complex molds, a spray-on mold release may be preferred. These sprays are designed to create an even, smooth barrier that helps prevent the glass from sticking. When using a spray, ensure that the application is uniform to avoid uneven surfaces on the finished piece.

3. Checking the Mold for Imperfections:

Before casting, inspect the mold for any cracks, chips, or other imperfections that could affect the final piece. Even small defects can cause issues during firing, leading to unwanted marks or structural weaknesses in the glass.

4. Loading the Mold with Glass:

The way you load the mold with glass depends on the design and desired outcome. You can use frit, chunks, or sheet glass, and each offers different effects. For example, layering different colors of frit can create intricate patterns and depth, while using sheet glass allows for more control over the final shape.

Casting with Frit and Glass Chunks

Frit and glass chunks are popular choices for kiln casting because they allow for a high degree of creativity and flexibility. Frit, which is finely ground glass, can be used to create detailed patterns and textures, while glass chunks add volume and structure to the cast piece.

1. Layering Frit:

Frit comes in various sizes, from fine powder to coarse granules, and can be layered to create different effects. Fine frit is ideal for adding color and subtle texture, while coarse frit can create a more dramatic, textured surface. When layering frit in the mold, start with a thin base layer and gradually build up to achieve the desired thickness and effect.

2. Using Glass Chunks:

Glass chunks, also known as cullet, are larger pieces of glass that can be strategically placed in the mold to create specific shapes and patterns. These chunks can be used alone or in combination with frit to add depth and dimension to the cast piece. When using glass chunks, consider their placement carefully, as they will flow and merge with surrounding glass during firing.

3. Mixing Colors and Effects:

One of the advantages of using frit and glass chunks is the ability to mix colors and create unique effects. You can blend different colors of frit to create gradients or use chunks of contrasting colors to add visual interest. Experimenting with different combinations will help you achieve the desired look for your project.

Firing Schedules for Kiln Casting

Firing schedules are critical to the success of a kiln casting project. The schedule dictates the temperature and timing of the firing process, which in turn affects the final appearance and structural integrity of the glass. A typical firing schedule for kiln casting includes several stages:

1. Ramp-Up (Heating):

The initial stage involves gradually increasing the temperature inside the kiln. A slow ramp-up is essential to prevent thermal shock, which can cause the glass to crack. The rate of increase depends on the thickness and type of glass being used, but a common rate is around 200°F (93°C) per hour.

2. Soak (Holding):

Once the kiln reaches the target temperature, it is held (soaked) at that temperature for a specified period. This allows the glass to fully melt and take on the shape of the mold. The soak time varies depending on the thickness of the glass and the desired effect but typically ranges from 10 minutes to several hours.

3. Ramp-Down (Cooling):

After the soak, the kiln temperature is gradually reduced to avoid thermal shock and to allow the glass to anneal properly. Annealing is a crucial process that relieves internal stresses within the glass, making it more durable and less prone to cracking. The cooling rate is usually slower than the ramp-up, often around 100°F (37°C) per hour.

4. Final Cooling:

Once the kiln reaches room temperature, the glass can be removed from the mold. However, it's important to be patient and allow the glass to cool fully inside the kiln before opening it. Premature cooling can result in thermal shock, which might cause the glass to crack or break. The final cooling stage is the most crucial in ensuring that the glass has properly annealed and is stable for long-term use.

7.3 Slumping Glass into Molds
Choosing the Right Slump Mold

Slumping is the process of heating flat glass until it becomes soft enough to conform to the shape of a mold placed beneath it. This technique is commonly used to create functional items like bowls, plates, and trays, as well as decorative objects. Choosing the right slump mold is essential to achieving the desired shape and quality in your final piece.

1. Types of Slump Molds:

- Ceramic Molds: Durable and reusable, ceramic molds are ideal for creating consistent, high-quality slumped glass pieces. They come in a wide variety of shapes, including basic forms like bowls and plates, as well as more complex designs with intricate details.
- Stainless Steel Molds: These molds are also reusable and are often preferred for their durability and ease of use. Stainless steel molds can be purchased in various shapes or custom-made for specific projects.
- Fiber Molds: Made from refractory fiber materials, these molds are lightweight and can be custom-shaped. Fiber molds are typically used for more experimental or one-of-a-kind pieces since they may not last as long as ceramic or stainless steel molds.

2. Selecting the Right Mold for Your Project:

The choice of mold depends on the design and functionality of your project. For a simple, everyday item like a bowl or plate, a standard ceramic mold may suffice. For more intricate or unique shapes, you might opt for a custom-made fiber or stainless steel mold. Consider the depth, curve, and overall shape of the mold to ensure it will produce the desired effect in your slumped glass piece.

Preparing the Mold for Slumping

Proper preparation of the slump mold is crucial to achieving a smooth, well-formed piece of slumped glass. The preparation process involves several steps to ensure the glass does not stick to the mold and that the final product is free of imperfections.

1. Applying Kiln Wash:

Similar to kiln casting, applying kiln wash to the surface of the mold is essential to prevent the glass from sticking. Ensure that the kiln wash is applied evenly and covers the entire surface that will come into contact with the glass. Allow the kiln wash to dry completely before placing the glass on the mold.

2. Positioning the Glass:

Carefully place the glass on top of the mold, ensuring that it is centered and balanced. Any misalignment can lead to uneven slumping, resulting in an asymmetrical or distorted final product. For larger or more complex pieces, you may need to use small pieces of glass or frit to help anchor the glass in place.

3. Cleaning the Glass:

Before slumping, it is important to clean the glass thoroughly to remove any dust, oils, or fingerprints that could mar the surface during firing. Use a glass cleaner or a mixture of water and vinegar, followed by a lint-free cloth to dry the glass.

Slumping Techniques: Draping, Sagging, and Bending

Slumping involves several techniques that can be used to achieve different effects and shapes. Understanding these techniques will allow you to expand your creative possibilities in glass fusing.

1. Draping:

In draping, the glass is placed over a mold, and as it heats, it softens and drapes over the edges, conforming to the mold's shape. This technique is often used to create shallow bowls, plates, and other vessels with soft curves. Draping can also be used to create more organic, flowing forms by allowing the glass to drape naturally over irregular molds or objects.

2. Sagging:

Sagging involves placing the glass over an opening in the mold, allowing gravity to pull the softened glass downward into the mold as it heats. This technique is useful for creating deeper forms, such as vases or goblets, where the glass needs to stretch into the mold's cavity. Sagging requires careful control of temperature and time to ensure that the glass doesn't over-sag, which could lead to thin or uneven walls.

3. Bending:

Bending is a technique used to shape glass into angular or curved forms without using a full mold. The glass is placed on top of supports or forms within the kiln, and as it heats, it bends to conform to the shape of the supports. This technique is often used to create functional items like bent glass shelves, wall hangings, or decorative architectural elements.

Each slumping technique offers unique possibilities, and by experimenting with different molds, temperatures, and timing, you can achieve a wide variety of shapes and effects in your glasswork.

7.4 Combining Slumping and Fusing
Creating Functional Art: Plates, Bowls, and Trays

Combining slumping with fusing allows you to create functional art pieces that are both beautiful and practical. By fusing glass into a flat sheet and then slumping it into a mold, you can create items like plates, bowls, and trays that are perfect for everyday use or as decorative pieces.

1. Designing Your Piece:

Start by designing the fused glass component of your piece. Consider the colors, patterns, and textures you want to incorporate, and how they will appear once the piece is slumped into shape. For functional items, it's important to consider the practicality of the design—sharp edges or uneven surfaces could make the piece less usable.

2. Fusing the Glass:

Once you've designed your piece, fuse the glass to create a flat sheet. This sheet will serve as the base for your slumped item. Use the techniques discussed in earlier chapters to achieve the desired design, color, and texture. After fusing, allow the glass to cool and anneal before moving on to the slumping process.

3. Slumping the Fused Glass:

After the fused glass has cooled, place it on top of your chosen slump mold. Carefully center the glass to ensure an even slump. Follow the appropriate slumping schedule, gradually heating the glass until it conforms to the mold's shape. After the glass has slumped, allow it to cool slowly in the kiln to avoid thermal shock.

Slumping After Fusing: Achieving Complex Shapes

Slumping after fusing is a powerful technique that allows you to create complex shapes and forms that would be difficult to achieve through fusing or slumping alone. By combining these techniques, you can produce highly detailed and intricate glass pieces that push the boundaries of traditional glass fusing.

1. Creating Multi-Layered Designs:

One approach to achieving complex shapes is to create multi-layered fused glass pieces before slumping. By layering different colors and types of glass, you can add depth and dimension to your piece. Once the layers have been fused, the entire piece can be slumped into a mold to create a three-dimensional form.

2. Using Complex Molds:

Complex molds, such as those with multiple curves, angles, or recesses, can be used to create intricate shapes in slumped glass. When using a complex mold, it's important to monitor the slumping process closely to ensure that the glass conforms to the mold without over-slumping or distorting.

3. Combining Multiple Molds:

For even more intricate shapes, you can combine multiple molds in a single firing. This technique involves slumping the glass in stages, moving it from one mold to another to create a compound shape. This process requires careful planning and precise control of the kiln schedule to avoid damaging the glass.

Troubleshooting Slumping Issues: Avoiding Distortion and Stress

Slumping glass into molds can sometimes result in issues such as distortion, uneven slumping, or stress fractures. Understanding the causes of these problems and how to avoid them will help you achieve better results in your glass fusing projects.

1. Preventing Distortion:

Distortion occurs when the glass slumps unevenly, often due to incorrect placement on the mold or uneven heating. To prevent distortion, ensure that the glass is properly centered on the mold and that the kiln is heating evenly. Avoid rushing the slumping process—slow, controlled heating is key to achieving a smooth, even slump.

2. Managing Stress in the Glass:

Stress in the glass can lead to cracks or fractures, particularly during the cooling process. To minimize stress, follow a proper annealing schedule that gradually reduces the kiln temperature, allowing the glass to cool slowly and evenly. Avoid opening the kiln too early, as rapid cooling can shock the glass and cause it to crack.

3. Correcting Slumping Issues:

If you encounter issues during slumping, such as incomplete slumping or bubbles in the glass, there are a few techniques you can use to correct the problem. In some cases, re-slumping the glass at a slightly higher temperature may resolve the issue. For bubbles, try adjusting the firing schedule to allow for a longer soak time at a lower temperature, which can help the bubbles rise to the surface and dissipate.

7.5 Casting with Lost Wax Techniques
Introduction to Lost Wax Casting for Glass

The lost wax casting technique, also known as cire perdue, is an ancient method used to create detailed sculptures and intricate designs in metal and glass. In glass fusing, lost wax casting involves creating a model in wax, which is then encased in a mold material such as plaster. The wax is melted away, leaving a cavity in the shape of the original model, which is then filled with glass and fired in a kiln.

Lost wax casting is particularly useful for creating highly detailed, one-of-a-kind glass pieces. The technique allows for precise control over the final shape and surface texture, making it a popular choice for artists who want to push the boundaries of glass fusing.

Creating Detailed Sculptures with Glass Casting

1. Designing the Wax Model:

The first step in lost wax casting is designing and creating the wax model. This model can be sculpted by hand or created using molds. Wax is a versatile material that can be carved, shaped, and textured to create intricate details. It's important to remember that the wax model will be an exact replica of the final glass piece, so take your time to perfect the design.

2. Making the Mold:

Once the wax model is complete, it's encased in a mold material such as plaster or investment. This material must be able to withstand the high temperatures of the kiln and accurately capture the fine details of the wax model. The mold is built up in layers, with each layer being carefully applied to avoid trapping air bubbles or creating weak spots.

3. Burning Out the Wax:

After the mold has been fully applied and allowed to dry, the wax is melted out, leaving a cavity in the shape of the model. This process is known as the "burnout" and is typically done in a kiln. The mold is slowly heated to a temperature that causes the wax to melt and flow out, leaving a clean, empty space ready to be filled with glass.

Firing and Finishing Cast Glass Pieces

1. Filling the Mold with Glass:

The empty mold cavity is filled with glass, which can be in the form of frit, powder, or chunks, depending on the desired effect. Careful attention must be paid to the type and placement of the glass to ensure even melting and filling of the mold. The mold is then placed in the kiln, where it is slowly heated until the glass melts and flows into the cavity, taking on the shape of the original wax model.

2. Firing the Mold:

The firing schedule for lost wax casting is similar to other kiln casting processes but often requires a longer soak time to ensure that the glass fully fills the mold. The temperature must be carefully controlled to avoid over-firing, which could cause the glass to lose detail or develop unwanted textures. After the glass has fully melted and taken on the shape of the mold, the kiln is gradually cooled to anneal the glass and prevent stress fractures.

3. Removing the Mold and Finishing the Piece:

Once the glass has cooled, the mold material is carefully removed, revealing the finished glass piece. Depending on the complexity of the mold and the fragility of the glass, this can be a delicate process. Any remaining mold material can be cleaned off using a combination of water, brushes, and gentle abrasive techniques.

4. Coldworking and Polishing:

The final step in the lost wax casting process is coldworking, which involves refining the surface of the glass and polishing it to a high sheen. This can include grinding down any rough edges, sanding the surface to remove imperfections, and polishing to achieve a smooth, glossy finish. Coldworking tools such as diamond pads, grinders, and polishers are typically used to achieve the desired result.

5. Displaying and Preserving the Cast Piece:

Once the piece is finished, it can be displayed as a standalone sculpture or incorporated into a larger artwork. Proper care and maintenance are important to preserve the integrity of the glass, including regular cleaning and avoiding exposure to extreme temperatures or harsh chemicals.

CHAPTER SEVEN
DISPLAYING AND SELLING YOUR WORK

8.1 Finishing Your Glass Pieces

Creating beautiful fused glass art is only part of the journey; finishing your pieces to a professional standard is crucial to presenting your work in the best possible light. This section will guide you through the essential steps of final coldworking, polishing, cleaning, and adding functional elements like hangers, stands, and frames to make your art ready for display and sale.

Final Coldworking for a Professional Finish

Coldworking refers to the process of refining and finishing glass pieces after they have been fired. This step is critical to achieving a professional look and feel. The goal is to smooth out rough edges, correct any imperfections, and enhance the overall appearance of your piece.

Start by evaluating the edges of your glass piece. After firing, edges may be sharp or uneven. Use a glass grinder to smooth out these edges, taking care to maintain the integrity of the piece's shape. For intricate designs, a diamond file can be used for more precise work. It's essential to work slowly and methodically, applying even pressure to avoid chipping the glass.

Once the edges are smooth, the next step is to polish the glass to bring out its natural shine. There are several methods for polishing, depending on the desired finish. A lap wheel is often used for a high-gloss finish, but for smaller or more delicate pieces, hand polishing with a cerium oxide

117

polish on a felt wheel can be effective. The polishing process not only enhances the aesthetic appeal of the glass but also strengthens the piece by removing microscopic imperfections that could lead to cracks over time.

Polishing and Cleaning Your Glass Art

After the coldworking process, the glass should be thoroughly cleaned to remove any residues from grinding and polishing. Even small particles of glass dust can mar the final appearance of your piece. Use a soft brush or compressed air to remove loose debris, followed by a thorough wash with warm water and a gentle glass cleaner. It's important to dry the glass completely with a lint-free cloth to prevent water spots.

For added shine and protection, consider applying a glass sealant. This not only gives your piece a lustrous finish but also helps protect it from environmental factors like dust and fingerprints. When cleaning fused glass that has multiple layers or intricate designs, pay special attention to the crevices, as these areas can easily trap dirt and residues.

Adding Hangers, Stands, and Frames

Displaying your glass art effectively requires the right support structures. For wall-mounted pieces, secure hangers are essential. There are several methods for adding hangers, depending on the weight and design of your piece. Small, lightweight pieces can be hung using adhesive hangers specifically designed for glass. For larger or heavier pieces, you may need to attach metal hangers directly to the glass using a strong epoxy adhesive.

Stands are another excellent option for displaying glass art, especially for three-dimensional or free-standing pieces. Custom-made stands can be designed to complement the shape and style of your work, enhancing its overall presentation. Metal stands are popular due to their durability and sleek appearance, but wooden stands can also provide a warm, organic contrast to the glass.

If you prefer to frame your work, choose a frame that enhances rather than detracts from the piece. The frame should be sturdy enough to support the glass but not so heavy that it overwhelms the artwork. Consider using shadow boxes for pieces with depth, or acrylic frames for a modern, minimalist look.

8.2 Photographing Glass Art

Photography is a vital tool in the glass artist's repertoire, especially when it comes to sharing your work with a wider audience online or in print. However, photographing glass can be challenging due to its reflective and transparent nature. In this section, we'll explore techniques for capturing the beauty of glass art in photos, from lighting strategies to tips for creating a professional portfolio.

Tips for Capturing the Beauty of Glass

The first step in photographing glass art is choosing the right environment. Natural light is ideal because it provides a soft, even illumination that enhances the colors and textures of the glass. If natural light isn't available, use softbox lights to mimic daylight. Avoid direct overhead lighting, as it can create harsh shadows and glare on the glass surface.

When positioning your glass piece for photography, consider the background carefully. A plain, neutral background is often the best choice, as it allows the glass to stand out without distraction. For transparent or translucent pieces, a black or dark background can create stunning contrast, highlighting the contours and colors of the glass. Conversely, opaque pieces may benefit from a white or light background to enhance their brightness.

One of the biggest challenges in photographing glass is managing reflections. To minimize unwanted reflections, position your lights at a 45-degree angle to the glass, and use a polarizing filter on your camera lens. This filter helps reduce glare and enhances the colors of the glass, making them appear more vibrant. Additionally, using diffusers on your lights can soften the light and further reduce reflections.

Lighting Techniques for Glass Photography

Lighting is crucial in glass photography because it can make or break the final image. The goal is to illuminate the glass evenly while avoiding hotspots and harsh shadows. As mentioned, softbox lights or natural light are ideal for achieving this effect. If you're working with artificial lights, experiment with different angles and distances to find the setup that best flatters your piece.

Backlighting is another technique that can be particularly effective with glass. By placing a light source behind the glass, you can create a glowing effect that accentuates the transparency and color of the piece. This technique works especially well with glass that has layers or internal patterns, as it brings out the depth and complexity of the design.

For pieces with intricate details or texture, consider using side lighting to highlight these features. By angling the light from the side, you can create subtle shadows that emphasize the texture and add dimension to the photograph. This approach is particularly useful for pieces with etched or embossed surfaces.

Preparing Photos for Portfolio and Online Sales

Once you've captured high-quality images of your glass art, it's time to prepare them for your portfolio or online store. Start by selecting the best shots that showcase the piece from different angles, ensuring that the images are sharp and well-lit. Editing software can be used to adjust the brightness, contrast, and color balance to match the actual appearance of the piece.

When preparing photos for online use, consider the platform where they will be displayed. For social media, square or vertical formats often work best, while horizontal images are ideal for websites and online stores. Make sure to resize the images appropriately to ensure fast loading times without compromising quality.

For a professional portfolio, organize your images in a way that tells a story. Group similar pieces together, and include close-ups of intricate details alongside full views of each piece. If you're selling online, each product listing should include multiple images that show the piece from different angles, along with a description that highlights its unique features.

8.3 Selling Your Glass Creations

Turning your passion for glass fusing into a source of income is a rewarding endeavor, but it requires careful planning and strategy. In this section, we'll cover essential tips for pricing your work, setting up an online store, and successfully selling at craft fairs and art shows.

Pricing Your Work: Factors to Consider

Pricing your glass art can be one of the most challenging aspects of selling your work. It's important to strike a balance between covering your costs, compensating yourself for your time and effort, and remaining competitive in the market. Start by calculating the cost of materials, including glass, tools, and any additional supplies like molds or frames. Don't forget to factor in overhead costs such as studio rent, utilities, and equipment maintenance.

Next, consider the time and skill involved in creating each piece. More complex or labor-intensive works should be priced higher to reflect the effort and expertise required. It can be helpful to keep track of the hours spent on each piece and assign an hourly rate for your work. Be sure to also consider the uniqueness and artistic value of your work; pieces that are one-of-a-kind or feature advanced techniques may justify a higher price.

Researching the market is also crucial. Look at what other glass artists with similar styles and skill levels are charging for their work. This will give you a sense of where your pricing fits within the broader market. However, it's important not to undervalue your work in an attempt to be competitive. Pricing too low can devalue your art and make it difficult to cover your costs.

Setting Up an Online Store: Platforms and Tips

An online store is a powerful tool for reaching a global audience and selling your glass creations. Several platforms are available, each with its own features and benefits. Etsy is a popular choice for handmade goods, offering a user-friendly interface and a large community of buyers interested in unique, artisanal items. Shopify provides more customization options and scalability, making it ideal for artists who plan to grow their business. Other platforms like Big Cartel or Squarespace also offer e-commerce solutions tailored to small businesses and artists.

When setting up your online store, focus on creating a cohesive and professional brand. Choose a store name that reflects your artistic style and vision, and design a logo that can be used across your website and social media profiles. Organize your products into categories to make it easy for customers to browse your offerings. Each product listing should include high-quality images, detailed descriptions, and clear pricing information.

Don't forget to optimize your store for search engines (SEO). Use relevant keywords in your product titles and descriptions to improve your visibility in search results. For example, include terms like "fused glass art," "handmade glass jewelry," or "custom glass decor" to attract buyers who are searching for these specific items.

Selling at Craft Fairs and Art Shows

In addition to online sales, craft fairs and art shows provide valuable opportunities to showcase your work in person and connect with potential customers. Preparing for a successful show requires careful planning and attention to detail.

Start by researching events that align with your target audience and artistic style. Local craft fairs, artisan markets, and art festivals are great places to begin. Apply early, as spots can fill up quickly, and make sure your booth presentation is professional and inviting.

Your booth should reflect your brand and showcase your work effectively. Invest in quality display materials, such as stands, tables, and lighting, to highlight your pieces. Arrange your work in a way that draws people in, using height and layers to create visual interest. Consider offering a range of price points to appeal to different buyers, from smaller, affordable items like pendants or coasters to larger, more expensive pieces like wall art or sculptures.

Engage with visitors by sharing the story behind your work and explaining your creative process. This personal connection can make a significant difference in whether a visitor decides to make a purchase. Be prepared to handle transactions efficiently by accepting multiple forms of payment, including credit cards and mobile payments.

8.4 Building a Brand as a Glass Artist

Building a strong brand is essential for standing out in the competitive world of glass art. Your brand is not just your logo or store name; it's the overall impression you create with your work, marketing, and customer interactions. This section will guide you through developing a signature style, marketing your work, and networking with other artists and industry professionals.

Developing a Signature Style

Your signature style is what sets you apart from other glass artists and makes your work instantly recognizable. It's the unique combination of techniques, colors, and designs that you consistently use in your creations. Developing a signature style takes time and experimentation, but it's a crucial step in building a successful brand.

Start by exploring different techniques and materials to find what resonates with you. Pay attention to the types of projects that excite you the most and the feedback you receive from others. Over time, patterns will emerge in your work, whether it's a particular color palette, a recurring motif, or a preferred method of fusing. Once you identify these elements, focus on refining and evolving them into a cohesive style.

While it's important to develop a recognizable style, don't be afraid to innovate and experiment within that framework. Your style should evolve as you grow as an artist, incorporating new influences and ideas while maintaining a consistent identity.

Marketing Your Work: Social Media, Websites, and Galleries

Effective marketing is key to building your brand and reaching a wider audience. Social media platforms like Instagram, Facebook, and Pinterest are powerful tools for promoting your work and connecting with potential customers. Regularly post high-quality images of your pieces, behind-the-scenes glimpses of your creative process, and updates on upcoming shows or product releases. Use hashtags relevant to glass art and your specific niche to increase visibility.

Your website is another essential marketing tool. It should serve as both a portfolio and an online store, showcasing your best work and making it easy for visitors to learn about your artistic journey and purchase your pieces. Include an "About" page that tells your story and explains your creative process, as well as a blog or news section where you can share insights, tips, and updates with your audience.

In addition to online marketing, consider approaching local galleries to display your work. Galleries can provide valuable exposure and lend credibility to your brand. When submitting your work to a gallery, prepare a professional portfolio that includes high-quality images, a biography, an artist statement, and details about your pricing and availability. Building relationships with gallery owners and curators can also lead to opportunities for solo exhibitions, collaborations, and increased sales.

Networking with Other Artists and Industry Professionals

Networking is a crucial aspect of building your brand and growing your career as a glass artist. Connecting with other artists, gallery owners, suppliers, and industry professionals can lead to collaborations, exhibitions, and valuable advice.

Join local and national glass art organizations to meet fellow artists and stay informed about industry events and trends. Attend workshops, conferences, and art fairs to expand your network and learn from others in the field. Social media is also a valuable tool for networking; engage with other artists and industry professionals by commenting on their posts, sharing their work, and participating in online discussions.

Building a strong network can open doors to new opportunities and provide support as you navigate the challenges of being a professional artist. Collaborations with other artists can lead to innovative projects that combine different techniques and styles, while relationships with gallery owners and curators can help you secure exhibitions and expand your audience.

8.5 Protecting Your Art: Legal Considerations

As you build your brand and sell your glass art, it's important to understand the legal aspects of your business. Protecting your intellectual property, navigating contracts, and managing the financial side of your art business are all essential components of long-term success.

Copyright and Intellectual Property

As an artist, your work is protected by copyright from the moment it is created. Copyright gives you the exclusive right to reproduce, distribute, and display your work. However, it's important to understand the scope and limitations of copyright protection.

Copyright does not protect ideas, techniques, or concepts, but rather the specific expression of those ideas in your work. For example, while you can't copyright the concept of fused glass jewelry, you can copyright a particular design that you've created.

To further protect your work, consider registering your copyright with the appropriate government agency. While registration is not required, it provides legal benefits, including the ability to seek statutory damages and attorney's fees in case of infringement.

Licensing Your Designs

Licensing your designs can be a lucrative way to expand your income stream and reach a wider audience. Licensing involves granting permission to a third party to reproduce and sell your work in exchange for a fee or royalty. This can be done with individual designs or an entire collection.

When entering into a licensing agreement, it's important to clearly define the terms of use, including the scope of the license (e.g., exclusive or non-exclusive), the duration of the agreement, and the compensation structure. It's also important to specify how the licensed work will be attributed and any limitations on its use.

Consulting with a legal professional who specializes in intellectual property can help you navigate the complexities of licensing and ensure that your interests are protected.

Navigating Contracts and Commissions

Contracts are an essential tool for protecting your rights and interests when working with clients, galleries, or collaborators. A well-drafted contract should clearly outline the terms of the agreement, including the scope of work, payment terms, deadlines, and any specific requirements or expectations.

When working on a commission, a contract is particularly important to ensure that both you and the client have a clear understanding of the project's details. The contract should include a description of the work to be created, the timeline for completion, the payment schedule, and any provisions for changes or revisions.

It's important to review and understand all terms of a contract before signing. If you have any concerns or questions, consult with a legal professional to ensure that the agreement is fair and protects your interests.

Understanding Tax Implications for Art Sales

As a professional artist, it's important to understand the tax implications of selling your work. Income from art sales is generally considered taxable, and you may be required to report it as self-employment income. This means you'll need to keep detailed records of your sales, expenses, and any business-related deductions.

You may also be required to collect and remit sales tax on your sales, depending on your location and the nature of your business. Sales tax regulations vary by jurisdiction, so it's important to understand the rules that apply to you.

Consulting with a tax professional who specializes in working with artists and small businesses can help you navigate the complexities of tax reporting and ensure that you comply with all applicable regulations.

CHAPTER EIGHT
MAINTENANCE AND TROUBLESHOOTING

9.1 Caring for Your Kiln

Regular Kiln Maintenance: Cleaning, Inspecting, and Replacing Parts

Maintaining your kiln is crucial to ensuring the longevity of your equipment and the success of your glass fusing projects. Regular maintenance begins with routine cleaning, which should be done after each use. Start by allowing the kiln to cool completely before cleaning. Use a soft brush to remove any debris or glass particles from the kiln's interior, being careful not to damage the kiln's delicate elements or thermocouples.

Inspecting your kiln regularly helps to catch potential problems early. Check the kiln's interior for any signs of damage, such as cracks in the bricks or worn-out elements. If you notice discoloration or physical damage to the kiln's walls, it might be time to replace those parts. The kiln's thermocouple, which measures temperature, is particularly susceptible to wear and tear and should be checked periodically. Replacing worn parts before they fail can save you from costly repairs and ensure consistent firing results.

Troubleshooting Common Kiln Issues

Even with regular maintenance, issues can arise with your kiln. Some common problems include uneven heating, failed firings, and error messages on digital controllers. Uneven heating often results from worn-out elements or issues with the kiln's insulation. To address this, check the condition of the heating elements and replace them if necessary. If the insulation is compromised, it may need to be repaired or replaced to restore even heat distribution.

Digital kilns can sometimes display error codes, indicating problems with the kiln's components or wiring. Consult your kiln's manual for a list of error codes and their meanings. Most issues can be resolved by resetting the kiln's controller or replacing faulty parts, such as the thermocouple or relays. If the problem persists, it may be time to contact the manufacturer or a professional technician for further assistance.

Extending the Life of Your Kiln: Best Practices

To maximize the lifespan of your kiln, it's essential to follow best practices in its operation and care. Avoid firing your kiln at maximum temperature limits too frequently, as this can shorten the life of the elements and other components. Instead, use the appropriate firing schedule for your glass projects and allow the kiln to cool gradually between firings.

Proper ventilation is also crucial to prolonging your kiln's life. Ensure that your kiln is placed in a well-ventilated area to prevent the buildup of fumes and heat, which can damage both the kiln and your workspace. Additionally, always use a kiln wash on shelves and molds to prevent glass from sticking and causing damage to the kiln's interior.

Finally, consider investing in a kiln cover or blanket when your kiln is not in use. This simple step can protect the kiln from dust, debris, and accidental damage, keeping it in top condition for your next project.

9.2 Glass Fusing Issues and Solutions

Tackling Common Problems: Cracks, Bubbles, and Devitrification

Cracks, bubbles, and devitrification are among the most common challenges in glass fusing. Cracks typically occur when the glass cools too quickly, leading to thermal stress. To avoid this, ensure that your kiln's annealing schedule is appropriate for the thickness and type of glass being used. Slow, controlled cooling is essential to prevent stress fractures.

Bubbles in fused glass can be caused by several factors, including trapped air between layers, contaminants on the glass surface, or an overly rapid firing schedule. To minimize bubbles, thoroughly clean your glass before fusing and consider using a bubble squeeze, which is a slow rise to a moderate temperature followed by a hold period, allowing trapped air to escape before full fusing.

Devitrification, or the crystallization of glass, occurs when the glass surface loses its smooth, shiny appearance and becomes dull and rough. This is often due to over-firing or extended hold times at high temperatures. Prevent devitrification by using clean glass, avoiding prolonged exposure to high temperatures, and considering the application of a devitrification spray, which can help maintain a smooth surface.

Understanding Why Glass Sometimes Misbehaves

Understanding the behavior of glass during firing is key to troubleshooting issues. Glass expands when heated and contracts when cooled, and different types of glass expand at different rates. This is measured by the coefficient of expansion (COE). When incompatible glasses are fused together, they cool at different rates, leading to stress and cracking. Always use glass with the same COE to ensure compatibility.

Another factor to consider is the glass's thickness. Thicker pieces require longer annealing times to cool evenly, while thinner pieces are more prone to warping if not properly supported during firing. Additionally, contamination from oils, fingerprints, or dirt can cause unexpected reactions during firing, leading to defects in the final piece.

Correcting Mistakes: When to Start Over vs. When to Repair

Not all mistakes in glass fusing require starting over. Minor cracks or surface flaws can often be repaired by refiring the piece with a slightly adjusted schedule. For example, a crack might be healed by a slower ramp-up to the annealing temperature, followed by a longer soak at that temperature. Surface imperfections like bubbles or devitrification can sometimes be smoothed out by fire polishing, a process where the piece is heated just enough to soften the surface without fully melting the glass.

However, in cases where the structural integrity of the piece is compromised, or the aesthetic flaws are too significant, it may be best to start over. Salvaging usable glass from the failed piece can still be an option for future projects, ensuring that even mistakes become part of your creative process.

9.3 Repairing Broken Glass Pieces
Techniques for Fixing Cracks and Breaks

Repairing cracked or broken glass pieces requires a delicate approach. For small cracks, re-firing the piece at a lower temperature with a slow ramp-up can help heal the crack. Use a tack fuse schedule, which is a lower temperature fuse that softens the glass without melting it completely, to minimize further stress on the piece.

For more significant breaks, the best option might be to grind the edges of the broken pieces smooth and reassemble them on a new piece of glass before re-firing. This method can incorporate the break into the design, turning a flaw into a feature. In some cases, adding new elements like frit or stringers can help mask the break and create a cohesive final piece.

Re-Fusing Pieces to Salvage Your Work

Re-fusing is an effective way to salvage work that didn't turn out as expected. Start by assessing the piece to determine if it's structurally sound enough for another firing. If it is, clean the glass thoroughly to remove any oils or contaminants, then plan your re-firing schedule carefully.

When re-fusing, consider altering the design by adding new layers or elements, such as additional glass, frit, or inclusions. This not only hides flaws but also gives you a chance to reimagine the piece, potentially enhancing its original design. Be mindful of the firing schedule, adjusting it to accommodate the additional material and ensuring proper annealing to prevent further issues.

Cold Joining: Using Adhesives and Mechanical Fixes

Cold joining refers to methods of assembling glass pieces without firing them together in a kiln. This can be particularly useful for repairing broken pieces or adding elements to a finished work. Epoxy adhesives are commonly used for cold joining, especially those specifically formulated for glass, as they provide a strong bond while remaining clear and durable.

Mechanical fixes, such as using metal brackets, wires, or clamps, can also be employed to join glass pieces without adhesive. These methods not only repair the piece but can also add an interesting textural or structural element to the design. When using mechanical fixes, ensure that all edges are smooth and that the glass is securely held to prevent shifting or further damage.

9.4 Storing Glass and Materials

Proper Storage Techniques for Glass Sheets and Scraps

Proper storage of glass sheets and scraps is essential to maintaining the quality of your materials and ensuring they are ready for use when needed. Glass sheets should be stored vertically to prevent warping and cracking. Use sturdy racks or shelves designed to support the weight and size of the sheets, and keep them separated by dividers to avoid chipping the edges.

Scraps should be organized by color, type, and size in clearly labeled containers. Consider using clear plastic bins or drawers for easy identification and access. Keeping scraps organized not only saves space but also makes it easier to find the right piece for future projects. It's also a good idea to periodically sort through your scraps, discarding any unusable pieces to maintain an organized workspace.

Organizing Your Workspace for Efficiency

An organized workspace is key to working efficiently and safely in glass fusing. Start by designating specific areas for different tasks, such as cutting, grinding, and assembling.

Keep your tools and materials within easy reach of these workstations to minimize the time spent searching for items during your projects.

Invest in storage solutions like pegboards, shelves, and drawers to keep tools organized and off your work surfaces. Labeling your tools and storage containers can further enhance efficiency, ensuring everything has a designated place. Regularly clean and declutter your workspace to maintain a safe and productive environment.

Protecting Your Supplies from Damage and Contamination

Glass and other fusing materials are sensitive to contamination from dust, oils, and moisture. To protect your supplies, store glass sheets and finished pieces in a clean, dry environment. Avoid touching the glass surfaces with bare hands, as oils can transfer from your skin and affect the final outcome during firing. Use gloves or clean, lint-free cloths when handling glass.

For other materials like frit, stringers, and powders, ensure they are stored in airtight containers to prevent moisture absorption and contamination. If you work in a humid environment, consider using silica gel packs or dehumidifiers in your storage areas to maintain a dry atmosphere and protect your materials. Additionally, keep your kiln and other equipment covered when not in use to prevent dust and debris from settling on them, which could contaminate your glass during firing.

9.5 Long-Term Care of Fused Glass Art
Cleaning and Maintaining Finished Pieces

Proper care of your finished fused glass pieces is essential to preserving their beauty and integrity over time. Regular cleaning is crucial, but it must be done gently to avoid scratching or damaging the surface. Use a soft, lint-free cloth or microfiber towel for dusting and wiping your pieces. When more thorough cleaning is needed, a mixture of mild soap and water is usually sufficient. Avoid harsh chemicals or abrasive cleaners, as these can damage the glass or any applied finishes, such as paint or decals.

For pieces that have intricate textures or detailed patterns, use a soft brush to reach into crevices. After cleaning, rinse the glass with clean water and dry it thoroughly to prevent water spots or streaks. If your piece has metallic inclusions or other delicate elements, take extra care during cleaning to avoid causing damage.

Avoiding Damage from Environmental Factors

Environmental factors like sunlight, temperature fluctuations, and humidity can all impact the longevity of your fused glass art. Direct sunlight can cause certain colors to fade over time, particularly if the glass contains pigments that are sensitive to UV light. To protect your pieces, avoid displaying them in areas with prolonged sun exposure. If sunlight is unavoidable, consider applying a UV-protective coating to help preserve the colors.

Temperature fluctuations can also cause stress in the glass, especially if the piece has varying thicknesses or includes different types of glass. To avoid thermal shock, keep your glass art away from heat sources like fireplaces, radiators, or direct sunlight. Similarly, avoid placing glass pieces in areas with high humidity, as moisture can damage certain finishes or encourage the growth of mold or mildew on organic materials embedded in the glass.

Restoring and Repairing Old or Damaged Glass Art

Over time, even well-cared-for glass art may require restoration or repair. Surface scratches, chips, and other minor damage can often be repaired through polishing or re-firing. To polish out surface scratches, use a cerium oxide polishing compound with a felt wheel or pad. Apply the compound to the scratch and work it into the glass with gentle pressure until the scratch is no longer visible.

For deeper chips or cracks, more extensive repair methods may be needed. In some cases, grinding down the damaged area and re-firing the piece to smooth out the surface can restore the glass to its original condition. If re-firing is not an option, consider using clear epoxy resin to fill in chips or cracks, followed by careful sanding and polishing to blend the repair with the surrounding glass.

If your piece has suffered significant damage, such as a major break or multiple fractures, it may be worth consulting a professional glass artist or restorer. They can assess the damage and recommend the best course of action, whether that involves advanced repair techniques, reassembly, or even the creation of a new piece inspired by the original.

CHAPTER NINE
THE FUTURE OF GLASS FUSING
10.1 Innovations in Glass Fusing
Emerging Technologies and Materials

The landscape of glass fusing is continuously evolving, driven by innovations in technology and the discovery of new materials. Emerging technologies are reshaping how artists approach glass fusing, enabling them to push boundaries and explore previously unimaginable possibilities.

1. Digital Design and CNC Technology: One of the most significant advancements is the integration of digital design and CNC (Computer Numerical Control) technology into the glass fusing process. Artists can now create intricate patterns and precise cuts using software and machines that translate digital designs into physical glass pieces. This technology allows for an unprecedented level of accuracy and detail, enabling complex designs that would be nearly impossible to achieve by hand.

2. Advanced Coatings and Inclusions: Another area of innovation is the development of advanced coatings and inclusions. These materials can be used to achieve unique effects in fused glass. For instance, dichroic coatings that shift colors depending on the angle of light add a dynamic element to glass art. New metallic inclusions and nanoparticle-based coatings offer artists a broader palette of textures and colors to work with, allowing for the creation of pieces with extraordinary visual depth and complexity.

3. High-Performance Kilns: Kiln technology has also seen significant advancements. Modern kilns are equipped with more sophisticated controllers that offer precise temperature

management, ensuring consistent results even with complex firing schedules. Some high-performance kilns are designed to heat and cool rapidly, reducing the overall time required for firing and increasing the efficiency of the studio.

4. Hybrid Materials: The introduction of hybrid materials, such as glass-ceramic composites, offers artists new creative avenues. These materials combine the best properties of glass and ceramics, such as the translucency of glass with the strength and durability of ceramics. This opens up possibilities for creating pieces that are both beautiful and functional, such as architectural elements or outdoor sculptures that can withstand the elements.

Advances in Kiln Design and Functionality

Kiln design has evolved significantly, with innovations aimed at improving efficiency, safety, and the overall user experience. Modern kilns are more versatile and accessible, catering to both beginners and professional artists.

1. Energy Efficiency: One of the key advances in kiln design is the focus on energy efficiency. Newer kilns are designed to retain heat better, reducing the amount of energy required to reach and maintain high temperatures. Insulation materials have improved, and some kilns now feature dual-layer insulation that minimizes heat loss. Additionally, programmable controllers allow for more efficient firing schedules, optimizing energy use by adjusting the heating and cooling phases based on the specific requirements of the glass.

2. Enhanced Control Systems: Kilns now come equipped with advanced control systems that provide artists with greater control over the firing process. Digital controllers allow for the programming of complex firing schedules,

including multiple ramp-up and cool-down phases. Some kilns offer remote monitoring and control via smartphone apps, enabling artists to adjust settings and monitor progress even when they are away from the studio.

3. Multi-Zone Heating: Another innovation is the development of multi-zone heating systems in kilns. These systems allow for different parts of the kiln to be heated at varying temperatures, which is particularly useful when fusing pieces of varying thicknesses or compositions. Multi-zone heating ensures more uniform results and reduces the risk of stress fractures or warping.

4. Safety Features: Safety has also been a focus of recent kiln innovations. Modern kilns are equipped with features such as automatic shut-off systems, overheat protection, and improved ventilation to ensure safe operation. These features make kilns more user-friendly and reduce the risk of accidents in the studio.

New Techniques and Trends in Glass Art

As technology and materials continue to evolve, so do the techniques and trends in glass fusing. Artists are constantly experimenting with new methods to achieve novel effects and push the boundaries of what is possible in glass art.

1. Reactive Glass Techniques: Reactive glass, which changes color when combined with other glass types during firing, has become increasingly popular. Artists use this technique to create unexpected and organic patterns that can add a unique element to their work. The unpredictability of reactive glass adds a level of excitement and challenge, as the final result is often a surprise.

2. Casting and Slumping: The combination of casting and slumping techniques is another trend gaining momentum.

Artists are using these methods to create complex, three-dimensional forms that go beyond the traditional flat pieces associated with glass fusing. By casting glass into molds and then slumping it over forms, artists can create sculptures, vessels, and other objects with intricate shapes and textures.

3. Mixed Media Integration: The integration of mixed media is a growing trend in contemporary glass art. Artists are combining glass with other materials, such as metal, wood, and fabric, to create multi-dimensional works that challenge traditional perceptions of glass as a medium. This approach allows for greater experimentation and the creation of pieces that are rich in texture and contrast.

4. Digital Printing on Glass: Digital printing on glass is another technique that is gaining popularity. This method allows artists to transfer detailed images and patterns onto glass surfaces with high precision. Digital printing opens up new possibilities for creating custom designs, portraits, and even reproductions of photographs on glass.

5. Environmental and Social Commentary: Many contemporary glass artists are using their work to address environmental and social issues. By incorporating recycled materials and themes related to sustainability, artists are creating pieces that not only showcase technical skill but also provoke thought and raise awareness. This trend reflects a broader movement in the art world towards using art as a platform for activism and change.

10.2 Sustainable Practices in Glass Fusing
Eco-Friendly Materials and Recycled Glass

Sustainability is becoming an increasingly important consideration in glass fusing, as artists and manufacturers seek to reduce their environmental impact. The use of eco-friendly materials and recycled glass is at the forefront of this movement.

1. Recycled Glass: One of the most straightforward ways to practice sustainability in glass fusing is by using recycled glass. Artists can source glass from discarded bottles, windows, and other glass products, giving new life to materials that would otherwise end up in landfills. Recycled glass can be melted down and reformed, allowing for creative experimentation with colors and textures. While working with recycled glass can present challenges, such as varying COEs, the environmental benefits and unique aesthetic qualities make it a rewarding practice.

2. Lead-Free and Non-Toxic Materials: Another aspect of sustainability is the use of lead-free and non-toxic materials. Traditional glass fusing materials can contain harmful substances that are released during firing, posing risks to both the environment and the artist. Lead-free glass and non-toxic adhesives, coatings, and paints offer safer alternatives without compromising on quality or artistic potential.

3. Eco-Friendly Kiln Wash and Mold Releases: Kiln wash and mold releases are essential for protecting molds and kiln shelves during firing, but traditional products can contain chemicals that are harmful to the environment. Eco-friendly alternatives are now available, made from natural and biodegradable ingredients that are just as effective as their conventional counterparts. Using these products helps reduce the overall environmental footprint of the glass fusing process.

Reducing Energy Consumption in the Studio

Energy consumption is a significant concern in glass fusing, given the high temperatures required for the process. Reducing energy use not only lowers costs but also minimizes the environmental impact of the craft.

1. Energy-Efficient Kilns: As mentioned earlier, modern kilns are designed to be more energy-efficient, with better insulation and more precise control systems. Choosing an energy-efficient kiln is one of the most impactful ways to reduce energy consumption in the studio. Additionally, using the kiln's full capacity by firing multiple pieces at once can optimize energy use.

2. Firing Schedules: Adjusting firing schedules can also help reduce energy consumption. By using slower ramp rates and shorter soak times, artists can achieve the desired results with less energy. It's essential to balance energy savings with the need for proper annealing to avoid compromising the quality of the final product.

3. Studio Insulation and Layout: The physical setup of the studio can also impact energy use. Proper insulation of the studio space helps maintain a stable temperature, reducing the need for additional heating or cooling. Additionally, organizing the workspace to minimize the movement of materials and tools can make the process more efficient and reduce the energy required for each project.

4. Alternative Energy Sources: Some artists are exploring the use of alternative energy sources to power their studios. Solar panels, for instance, can provide a renewable source of energy for running kilns and other equipment. While the initial investment in solar energy can be high, the long-term savings and environmental benefits make it a worthwhile consideration for those committed to sustainability.

Creating Art with a Minimal Environmental Footprint

Beyond material choices and energy use, there are other ways to minimize the environmental footprint of glass fusing.

1. Waste Reduction: Reducing waste is a critical component of sustainable glass fusing. Artists can minimize waste by carefully planning their projects to use materials efficiently, reusing scraps, and recycling any unused glass. Implementing a system for collecting and reusing water from glass cutting and grinding processes can also help reduce waste.

2. Sustainable Sourcing: Choosing materials that are sustainably sourced is another way to reduce environmental impact. This includes selecting glass from manufacturers that prioritize eco-friendly practices and using local materials to reduce the carbon footprint associated with transportation.

3. Green Studio Practices: Adopting green studio practices, such as reducing water and chemical use, conserving energy, and recycling materials, can make a significant difference. Simple changes, like switching to LED lighting and using environmentally friendly cleaning products, contribute to a more sustainable studio environment.

10.3 The Role of Glass Fusing in Contemporary Art

How Glass Artists are Pushing Boundaries

Glass fusing has become a powerful medium for contemporary artists looking to push the boundaries of traditional art forms. The unique properties of glass—its transparency, fluidity, and versatility—allow artists to explore new dimensions in their work, both literally and metaphorically.

1. Exploration of Scale: One way artists are pushing boundaries is through the exploration of scale. Large-scale installations, often created by fusing multiple glass panels together, challenge the traditional notion of glass as a delicate, small-scale medium. These monumental works can dominate a space, transforming entire environments with their presence. Conversely, artists are also creating incredibly detailed miniature pieces that invite viewers to engage closely with the work, often requiring careful attention to appreciate the intricate craftsmanship involved.

2. Innovative Use of Light: Light is an inherent part of glass art, and contemporary glass artists are using it in increasingly innovative ways. By experimenting with different thicknesses, transparencies, and colors, artists can manipulate how light interacts with their pieces, creating dynamic works that change depending on the viewer's perspective and the time of day. Some artists incorporate LED lighting or projectors to enhance these effects, making the interplay of light and glass a central element of the artwork.

3. Kinetic and Interactive Art: Another exciting development is the creation of kinetic and interactive glass art. Artists are integrating motion and viewer interaction into their pieces, using mechanisms that allow the glass to move or change form. These works invite viewers to engage directly with the art, challenging the passive role of the observer and making

the viewing experience a participatory event. The fusion of glass with other materials and technologies in these pieces underscores the medium's potential for innovation.

4. Narrative and Conceptual Art: Glass fusing is also being used to tell stories and explore conceptual themes. Artists are leveraging the material's ability to encapsulate, layer, and juxtapose imagery to create narrative-driven works that address social, political, and personal issues. The transparency of glass allows for the layering of images and symbols, creating complex compositions that can be read and interpreted in multiple ways. This narrative potential is being explored in both two-dimensional panels and three-dimensional sculptures.

The Intersection of Glass Art and Technology

The intersection of glass art and technology is a fertile ground for innovation, offering artists new tools and methods to expand their creative horizons.

1. Digital Fabrication and 3D Printing: Digital fabrication techniques, including 3D printing, are revolutionizing glass art. Artists can now design intricate patterns and forms using computer-aided design (CAD) software and then translate these designs into physical objects through 3D printing. While printing directly in glass is still a developing technology, 3D-printed molds and forms are being used in the kiln casting process to achieve complex shapes that would be difficult or impossible to create by hand.

2. Augmented Reality (AR) and Virtual Reality (VR): AR and VR technologies are opening up new possibilities for how glass art is experienced. Artists are using these tools to create virtual galleries where viewers can interact with glass art in a digital space, or to develop AR applications that overlay

digital imagery onto physical glass pieces, adding an extra layer of meaning or interaction. These technologies allow for the creation of hybrid works that exist both in the physical and digital realms, pushing the boundaries of what constitutes a work of art.

3. Advanced Imaging and Patterning Techniques: Technologies such as laser engraving, digital printing, and photolithography are enabling artists to achieve unprecedented levels of detail and precision in their glass work. These techniques can be used to transfer photographic images, intricate patterns, or even complex mathematical designs onto glass, opening up new avenues for artistic expression. The ability to reproduce detailed imagery on glass allows artists to combine traditional craftsmanship with modern technology, creating works that are both visually stunning and conceptually rich.

4. Integration with Smart Technologies: The integration of smart technologies into glass art is an emerging trend. Artists are exploring how glass can be combined with sensors, lights, and other electronic components to create responsive, interactive works. For example, glass pieces that change color or opacity in response to environmental factors, or sculptures that emit sound or light based on viewer interaction, are pushing the boundaries of what glass art can be. These smart glass works challenge the traditional static nature of art, creating dynamic pieces that evolve and interact with their surroundings.

Glass Fusing in Installation Art and Public Works

Glass fusing has found a prominent place in installation art and public works, where its unique properties can be fully exploited to create impactful, large-scale pieces.

1. Site-Specific Installations: Artists are creating site-specific installations that respond to the architecture and environment of a space. These installations often use the transparency and reflective qualities of glass to play with light and perception, transforming the way a space is experienced. Whether in a public plaza, a museum atrium, or a corporate headquarters, these installations can become focal points that engage viewers and invite contemplation.

2. Public Art and Civic Engagement: Glass fusing is also being used in public art projects that aim to engage communities and beautify public spaces. These projects often involve collaboration between artists, architects, and urban planners, resulting in works that are integrated into the fabric of the community. Fused glass murals, sculptures, and architectural elements can add color, light, and artistic expression to public spaces, making art accessible to a broader audience. These public works often address social and cultural themes, using the medium of glass to reflect the identity and history of the community.

3. Interactive and Immersive Experiences: In the realm of installation art, glass fusing is being used to create immersive experiences that envelop viewers in a sensory-rich environment. By combining glass with light, sound, and other media, artists can create installations that engage multiple senses, providing a deeply immersive experience. These installations often explore themes of nature, perception, and the human experience, using the material properties of glass to enhance the emotional and psychological impact of the work.

10.4 Inspiration from Master Glass Artists
Profiles of Renowned Glass Artists

The world of glass fusing is rich with master artists whose work has pushed the boundaries of the medium and inspired countless others. Understanding their contributions and techniques provides valuable insight into the potential of glass as an art form.

1. Dale Chihuly: Perhaps the most famous glass artist in the world, Dale Chihuly has revolutionized the art of glass with his large-scale installations and innovative techniques. Known for his vibrant, organic forms and use of color, Chihuly's work often blurs the line between sculpture and installation, transforming spaces with his dynamic glass creations. His approach to glass fusing, particularly in the creation of his "Persians" and "Seaforms" series, has inspired a generation of artists to explore the possibilities of working on a large scale and using glass as a medium for installation art.

2. Lino Tagliapietra: A master of Venetian glassmaking techniques, Lino Tagliapietra is renowned for his technical skill and innovative approach to glass art. His work combines traditional methods with modern aesthetics, resulting in pieces that are both visually stunning and technically complex. Tagliapietra's influence on the world of glass fusing is profound, as he has demonstrated the potential of combining fusing techniques with blown glass to create intricate, layered pieces that showcase the full range of glass's expressive possibilities.

3. Klaus Moje: Often considered the father of the studio glass movement in Australia, Klaus Moje was a pioneer in the use of fused glass as a medium for artistic expression. His work is characterized by bold, geometric patterns and a vibrant use of color. Moje's innovative techniques in glass fusing, particularly his use of color bars and pattern bars, have had a

lasting impact on the field. His commitment to experimentation and pushing the boundaries of what was possible with fused glass continues to inspire artists today.

4. Bertil Vallien: A Swedish artist known for his work in sand-cast glass, Bertil Vallien's approach to glass fusing is both poetic and innovative. His work often explores themes of mythology, identity, and the human condition, using glass as a medium for storytelling. Vallien's techniques in casting and fusing, particularly his use of inclusions and layered imagery, have expanded the narrative potential of glass art. His work serves as an inspiration for artists looking to explore the deeper, conceptual possibilities of glass fusing.

Analyzing Iconic Works in Fused Glass

Examining iconic works in fused glass offers valuable lessons in technique, composition, and the expressive potential of the medium. These works serve as benchmarks for excellence and creativity in glass fusing.

1. "Macchia Series" by Dale Chihuly: Chihuly's "Macchia Series" is a celebration of color and form. Each piece in the series is characterized by its vibrant, swirling patterns and organic shapes. The series demonstrates Chihuly's mastery of color application in glass fusing, using layers of glass frit and powders to achieve complex, multi-dimensional effects. The fluid, dynamic forms of the "Macchia Series" also highlight the possibilities of pushing the boundaries of traditional shapes in fused glass, creating pieces that seem to defy gravity and conventional expectations.

2. "Confluence of Memories" by Klaus Moje: This work by Klaus Moje is a stunning example of his use of color bars to create intricate, geometric patterns. "Confluence of Memories" is a large-scale fused glass panel that combines

hundreds of small, individually fused pieces to create a cohesive, visually striking composition. The piece is a testament to Moje's technical skill and his ability to transform simple shapes and colors into a complex, harmonious whole. It also illustrates the potential of fused glass to create large, impactful works that command attention in any space.

3. "Passage" by Bertil Vallien: Vallien's "Passage" is a powerful example of the narrative potential of fused glass. The piece is a cast and fused glass boat, filled with symbolic objects and figures. The translucency of the glass allows light to pass through, creating an ethereal, almost ghostly effect. "Passage" explores themes of journey, memory, and the passage of time, using the medium of glass to evoke a sense of mystery and contemplation. The work demonstrates how fused glass can be used to create narrative-driven pieces that resonate on an emotional and intellectual level.

4. "Reticello Vessels" by Lino Tagliapietra: Lino Tagliapietra's "Reticello Vessels" showcase his mastery of the reticello technique, a traditional Venetian glassmaking method that involves creating intricate, lattice-like patterns in glass. In these vessels, Tagliapietra combines blown glass with fused elements to create pieces that are both technically complex and visually stunning. The precise, delicate patterns in the glass highlight the potential of combining fusing and blowing techniques to create works that are rich in detail and craftsmanship.

Learning from the Masters: Techniques and Approaches

Studying the techniques and approaches of master glass artists provides valuable insights for those looking to advance their own skills in glass fusing.

1. Experimentation and Innovation: One common thread among master glass artists is their willingness to experiment and push the boundaries of traditional techniques. Whether it's Chihuly's bold use of color and form, Moje's innovative patterning, or Vallien's narrative-driven work, these artists have all embraced experimentation as a key part of their practice. Aspiring glass fusing artists can learn from this by not being afraid to try new things, make mistakes, and discover new possibilities in their work.

2. Attention to Detail: The work of master glass artists is often characterized by meticulous attention to detail. This can be seen in the precise patterns of Tagliapietra's vessels, the careful layering of color in Moje's panels, or the symbolic elements in Vallien's sculptures. For those looking to improve their glass fusing skills, focusing on the details— whether it's the way glass pieces are cut, how they are arranged before fusing, or how they are finished after firing— can make a significant difference in the quality of the final piece.

3. Understanding the Material: Master glass artists have a deep understanding of their material—how it behaves under different conditions, how it interacts with light, and how it can be manipulated to achieve the desired effect. This understanding comes from years of experience, but it can also be cultivated through careful observation and practice. Spending time experimenting with different types of glass, firing schedules, and techniques will help artists develop a deeper connection with the material and improve their ability to control the final outcome.

4. Embracing the Unexpected: Glass is a material that is often unpredictable, especially during the fusing process. Master artists like Chihuly and Vallien have learned to

embrace this unpredictability, using it to their advantage to create works that are dynamic and full of life. Aspiring glass artists can take a similar approach by being open to the unexpected and allowing the material to guide them in new and surprising directions.

157

CHAPTER TEN
RESOURCES FOR GLASS FUSING ARTISTS

11.1 Suppliers and Materials
Where to Buy Glass and Supplies

Finding the right suppliers is crucial for any glass fusing artist. Quality materials not only make your work easier but also ensure the longevity and durability of your creations. When looking for suppliers, consider both local and online options.

1. Local Suppliers:

Visiting local glass suppliers has its advantages. You can physically inspect the glass for any imperfections, choose from a wide range of colors and textures, and often get advice from experienced staff. Local suppliers often offer classes or workshops where you can learn new techniques and connect with other glass artists in your area. Look for art supply stores that specialize in glass or larger craft stores with a dedicated glass section.

2. Online Suppliers:

The internet offers a vast array of options for purchasing glass fusing materials. Online suppliers often provide a wider selection of glass types, tools, and specialty items that might be hard to find locally. Some popular online suppliers include Bullseye Glass Co., Delphi Glass, and Spectrum Glass. These websites offer everything from fusible glass sheets to kilns and accessories. Additionally, online shopping allows you to compare prices and read reviews from other artists, helping you make informed decisions.

Recommendations for Quality Tools and Equipment

When it comes to tools and equipment, investing in quality pays off in the long run. Here's a list of essential tools and equipment, along with recommendations for where to purchase them:

- Glass Cutters: A good glass cutter is a must. Look for carbide wheel cutters for longevity and precision. Toyo and Fletcher are reputable brands that offer reliable cutters.
- Running Pliers: These pliers help break the glass along scored lines with minimal effort. Make sure to choose a pair with adjustable tension for better control.
- Kilns: Your kiln is the heart of your glass fusing operation. Consider a kiln that offers programmable temperature control for precision. Paragon and Skutt are industry leaders, known for their durable and reliable kilns.
- Grinders: A grinder helps smooth out the edges of cut glass. Inland and Gryphon make durable grinders that are easy to use and maintain.

Finding Specialty Glass and Unique Materials

Specialty glass, such as dichroic glass or glass with embedded patterns, can add a unique touch to your work. These materials are often used for specific effects, such as creating jewelry or adding iridescence to a piece. Specialty glass is usually more expensive, so it's important to buy from reputable suppliers who can guarantee the quality and compatibility of the glass.

- Dichroic Glass: This glass has a thin, metallic film that creates a stunning color-changing effect. Coatings by

Sandberg (CBS) is a top supplier of dichroic glass, offering a wide range of colors and patterns.

- Reactive Glass: This type of glass changes color when combined with other materials, creating unique effects. Bullseye Glass Co. offers a variety of reactive glass options.
- Frit and Powders: Frit is crushed glass that can be used for texturing and coloring. Powders are finely ground glass used for delicate shading and blending. Reputable suppliers include Oceanside Glass & Tile and Spectrum Glass.

11.2 Learning and Inspiration

Recommended Books, Tutorials, and Online Courses

Education is key to mastering the art of glass fusing. Whether you're a beginner or an experienced artist, there are numerous resources available to help you improve your skills.

1. Books:

Several books are considered essential reading for glass fusing artists:

- "Contemporary Fused Glass" by Brad Walker: This book covers a wide range of techniques and projects, making it a valuable resource for both beginners and advanced artists.
- "Glass Fusing: Techniques & Designs" by Peter McGrain: McGrain's book is an excellent guide to the creative and technical aspects of glass fusing, including advanced techniques.

- "Kiln-Formed Glass: Beyond the Basics" by Boyce Lundstrom: This book delves into more complex techniques, perfect for artists looking to push their skills further.

2. Tutorials and Online Courses:

The internet is filled with tutorials that cover every aspect of glass fusing. Websites like YouTube, Skillshare, and Udemy offer both free and paid tutorials. These platforms allow you to learn at your own pace, with video demonstrations that make complex techniques easier to understand.

- YouTube Channels: Check out channels like Delphi Glass and Bullseye Glass for a variety of tutorials that range from basic to advanced techniques.
- Skillshare: This platform offers structured courses, often taught by experienced glass artists, that provide step-by-step guidance on specific projects.
- Udemy: Udemy offers courses that cover everything from the basics of glass cutting to advanced kiln techniques.

Visiting Glass Museums and Exhibitions

Museums and exhibitions are a great way to draw inspiration from the masters of glass art. Seeing the work of established artists up close can ignite new ideas and help you understand the possibilities of glass as a medium.

1. Glass Museums:

- Corning Museum of Glass (Corning, New York): One of the largest collections of glass art in the world, with pieces spanning centuries. The museum also offers live demonstrations and workshops.

- The Glass Museum (Tacoma, Washington): This museum showcases contemporary glass art and features a hot shop where you can watch glassblowers at work.
- European Glass Museums: Consider visiting glass museums in Murano, Italy, or the Glasmuseet Ebeltoft in Denmark for a glimpse into the history and craftsmanship of European glass artists.

2. Exhibitions:

Attending exhibitions, both local and international, can provide insights into current trends and techniques in glass fusing. Events like SOFA (Sculpture Objects Functional Art and Design) in Chicago or the British Glass Biennale are excellent opportunities to network and see the latest in glass art.

Connecting with Glass Artists Online and in Person

Building connections with other glass artists is invaluable for growth and inspiration. Whether through social media, forums, or local art groups, these connections can lead to collaborations, mentorships, and lasting friendships.

Online Communities:

- Facebook Groups: There are numerous Facebook groups dedicated to glass fusing where members share their work, ask questions, and offer advice. Groups like "Glass Fusing 101" or "Kiln-Formed Glass Artists" are great places to start.
- Glass Art Forums: Websites like Warm Glass and Fused Glass Projects offer forums where artists can discuss techniques, troubleshoot issues, and share tips.

- Instagram: Following glass artists on Instagram can provide daily inspiration and keep you connected with the latest trends in the glass art community.

In-Person Networking:

Attending workshops, classes, and glass art events in person allows you to meet other artists face-to-face. These interactions often lead to collaborations and new opportunities. Consider joining a local art league or attending a glass art conference, such as the Glass Art Society Conference, to expand your network.

11.3 Glass Fusing Communities and Networks
Joining Local and National Glass Art Groups

Being part of a glass art community can greatly enhance your experience as an artist. Local and national groups offer support, resources, and a sense of belonging to those passionate about glass fusing.

1. Local Glass Art Groups:

Joining a local glass art group can provide you with hands-on experience and immediate access to a community of like-minded individuals. These groups often organize workshops, group projects, and exhibitions that allow you to grow your skills and showcase your work.

2. National Glass Art Groups:

National organizations, such as the Glass Art Society (GAS), offer a broader network and more extensive resources. Membership in these organizations typically includes access to conferences, publications, and exclusive online content. Being part of a national group can also increase your exposure to potential clients and galleries.

Participating in Competitions and Shows

Entering competitions and participating in shows are excellent ways to gain recognition and validate your work. Competitions provide a platform for artists to showcase their skills, receive feedback from experts, and potentially win prizes that can further their careers.

1. Types of Competitions:

- Juried Exhibitions: These shows are curated by professionals in the field and offer a prestigious platform for emerging and established artists.
- Themed Competitions: Many competitions have specific themes, such as "Recycled Glass" or "Functional Art," allowing you to explore different facets of glass fusing.
- Online Competitions: These have become increasingly popular, allowing artists to submit their work digitally. They provide exposure to a global audience without the need to travel.

2. Preparing for a Show:

Participating in a show requires preparation, from creating a cohesive body of work to marketing your pieces effectively. Ensure your work is presented professionally, with clear labeling and artist statements that explain your process and inspiration.

Online Forums and Social Media Groups for Glass Artists

The digital age has made it easier than ever to connect with fellow artists across the globe. Online forums and social media groups provide spaces for glass artists to share their work, ask questions, and offer support.

1. Forums:

- Warm Glass: A forum dedicated to all things glass fusing, where artists of all levels can ask for advice, share their projects, and discuss new techniques.
- Fused Glass Projects: This forum focuses on sharing project ideas and step-by-step tutorials, making it a great resource for beginners and seasoned artists alike.

2. Social Media Groups:

- Facebook: Many Facebook groups cater to glass fusing artists, offering a space to share photos, discuss challenges, and celebrate successes.
- Instagram: Using hashtags like #glassfusing or #fusedglass connects you with a wider community of glass artists. Following popular glass artists and participating in challenges can also inspire your work.

11.4 Setting Up Your Glass Fusing Studio
Studio Design: Layout and Space Considerations

Setting up a functional and efficient glass fusing studio is essential for both safety and productivity. Whether you're converting a spare room, a garage, or setting up a dedicated studio space, thoughtful planning will ensure that your studio meets your creative needs.

1. Space Requirements:

- Work Areas: Ideally, your studio should have distinct areas for cutting glass, assembling pieces, and kiln firing. This separation helps prevent contamination and allows you to work more efficiently.

- Ventilation: Proper ventilation is critical, especially when working with kilns and potentially hazardous materials like glass powders or adhesives. Consider installing an exhaust fan or working in a well-ventilated area to keep the air clean and safe.
- Lighting: Good lighting is essential for detailed work. Natural light is ideal, but if that's not possible, ensure you have adequate overhead lighting and task lights for precision work.
- Storage: Glass sheets, tools, and supplies all need organized storage to keep your workspace tidy and safe. Use sturdy shelving, drawers, and bins to store your materials. Consider vertical storage racks for large glass sheets and compartmentalized storage for small tools and accessories.

2. Ergonomics:

- Workbenches: Your workbench should be at a comfortable height to prevent strain during long hours of cutting and assembling. Adjustable workbenches or standing desks can provide flexibility.
- Seating: If your work requires sitting, invest in a comfortable, adjustable chair that supports good posture.
- Safety Zones: Designate areas for potentially hazardous activities, such as kiln operation, and ensure these zones are free from clutter and have easy access to safety equipment.

Essential Tools and Equipment for Every Studio

Equipping your studio with the right tools is crucial for successful glass fusing. While some tools are essential, others can enhance your efficiency and the quality of your work.

1. Basic Tools:

- Glass Cutters: A reliable glass cutter is a must. Choose one with a comfortable grip and a durable cutting wheel.
- Running and Grozing Pliers: These tools help you control the breaking of glass along scored lines and refine the edges.
- Kiln: Your kiln is the centerpiece of your studio. Choose one that suits your project sizes and frequency of use. A programmable kiln with digital controls allows for precise temperature management, which is critical for successful fusing.
- Grinding Tools: A glass grinder smooths the edges of cut glass and allows for precise shaping. It's an essential tool for achieving clean, finished edges.
- Kiln Shelves and Kiln Wash: These protect the kiln floor from melted glass and provide a stable surface for your projects.

2. Advanced Tools:

- Ring Saw: A ring saw allows for intricate cuts and shapes that are difficult to achieve with a standard glass cutter.
- Glass Drill: For drilling holes in glass, such as for jewelry or hanging pieces, a glass drill with diamond-tipped bits is essential.

- Slumping Molds: These molds allow you to shape fused glass into three-dimensional forms, such as bowls or plates.
- Surface Treatments: Tools like sandblasters or acid etching kits can add texture and patterns to your glass pieces.

Tips for Organizing and Maintaining a Productive Workspace

A well-organized workspace not only boosts productivity but also ensures safety and efficiency in your glass fusing practice.

1. Organizing Materials:

- Glass Storage: Store glass sheets upright in racks to prevent breakage and allow for easy access. Smaller pieces can be stored in drawers or bins, sorted by color, size, or type.
- Tool Storage: Keep frequently used tools within easy reach. Pegboards, magnetic strips, or wall-mounted tool racks can help keep your tools organized and off your workbench.
- Supply Storage: Designate bins or drawers for frits, powders, stringers, and other small materials. Labeling containers helps you quickly find what you need during the creative process.

2. Maintaining Your Studio:

- Cleaning Routine: Regularly clean your work surfaces, tools, and equipment to remove glass dust and debris. This not only keeps your workspace tidy but also prevents contamination in your projects.

- Kiln Maintenance: Periodically inspect your kiln for signs of wear and tear. Replace kiln shelves or apply new kiln wash as needed to prevent glass from sticking during firing. Regularly check the kiln's heating elements and ensure that the kiln is operating at accurate temperatures.
- Safety Checks: Ensure that all safety equipment, such as fire extinguishers, first aid kits, and ventilation systems, are in good working order. Review your safety protocols regularly and make sure your workspace adheres to them.

3. Personalizing Your Studio:

- Creative Displays: Consider setting up an inspiration board or displaying some of your favorite glass pieces in your studio. This can provide motivation and spark new ideas during your creative process.
- Comfort Items: Personalize your studio with items that make the space comfortable and inviting, such as a good sound system for music or an area for breaks.

CONCLUSION
YOUR JOURNEY WITH GLASS FUSING

Reflecting on Your Growth as a Glass Artist

From Beginner to Advanced: Charting Your Progress

Embarking on the journey of glass fusing is like stepping into a world where creativity meets precision. When you first began, the idea of cutting, layering, and firing glass may have seemed daunting. However, as you practiced, the basics became second nature, and you started to see the transformation from raw materials to finished art. Reflecting on your progress, it's essential to recognize how far you've come. Each project, whether successful or a learning experience, has contributed to your growth as an artist. You've moved from simple fusing techniques to more complex creations, experimenting with different types of glass, molds, and firing schedules. Charting your progress allows you to appreciate the skills you've developed and the artistry you've honed.

Embracing the Challenges and Rewards of Glass Fusing

Glass fusing, like any art form, comes with its set of challenges. From mastering the delicate balance of kiln temperatures to overcoming unexpected outcomes, each obstacle is a stepping stone in your artistic journey. Embracing these challenges is crucial; they push you to refine your techniques and deepen your understanding of the medium. The rewards, however, are equally significant. The moment when you open the kiln to reveal a perfectly fused piece, or when you achieve a complex pattern that you've been working on, is immensely gratifying. These rewards fuel your passion and drive, reminding you why you embarked on this journey in the first place.

Setting Goals for Future Projects and Artistic Growth

As you reflect on your growth, it's important to set new goals to continue advancing your skills and creativity. Perhaps you want to tackle larger projects, experiment with advanced techniques like kiln casting or pâte de verre, or even explore the commercial side of glass fusing by selling your work. Setting clear, achievable goals will guide your artistic development and keep your passion for glass fusing alive. Consider joining workshops, participating in exhibitions, or collaborating with other artists to further enrich your journey. Remember, the key to growth is to continuously challenge yourself, take risks, and push the boundaries of what you can create.

Staying Inspired and Motivated
Finding Inspiration in Everyday Life

Inspiration for your glass art can come from the most unexpected places. The play of light through a window, the colors of a sunset, or the textures of natural elements can all spark new ideas for your glass creations. Keeping an open mind and staying observant in your daily life will help you find inspiration everywhere. Consider keeping a journal or sketchbook where you jot down ideas, colors, or patterns that catch your eye. These notes can serve as a valuable resource when you're planning your next project. By drawing inspiration from the world around you, your work will continue to evolve and reflect your unique perspective as an artist.

Continuing to Experiment and Take Risks

As you gain confidence in your glass fusing abilities, it's crucial to continue experimenting and taking risks. Trying new techniques, exploring different materials, and pushing the limits of what glass can do will keep your work fresh and exciting. Don't be afraid of failure—every experiment, whether it succeeds or not, teaches you something valuable. For instance, experimenting with color blends, texture creation, or multi-layered compositions can lead to unexpected and beautiful results. Remember, the most innovative and impactful art often comes from stepping outside of your comfort zone. By maintaining a spirit of curiosity and experimentation, you'll keep your passion for glass fusing alive and thriving.

Connecting with Other Artists for Mutual Support and Encouragement

Artistic journeys are often enriched by the connections you make with fellow artists. Whether through local workshops, online communities, or collaborative projects, engaging with other glass fusers can provide you with new perspectives, ideas, and encouragement. Sharing your experiences, discussing techniques, and even critiquing each other's work can be incredibly beneficial. These connections can also lead to collaborative projects that push your creativity in new directions. Surrounding yourself with a supportive network of artists can help you stay motivated, inspired, and continually growing in your craft.

The Endless Possibilities of Glass Fusing
Exploring New Techniques and Ideas

Glass fusing is a dynamic and ever-evolving art form with endless possibilities for exploration. As you continue your journey, challenge yourself to explore new techniques that you've yet to master. Whether it's experimenting with dichroic glass for dazzling effects, incorporating mixed media into your work, or delving into the complexities of kiln casting, there's always something new to learn. These new techniques not only expand your skill set but also open up new avenues for creative expression. Each new method you master becomes another tool in your artistic arsenal, allowing you to bring even more of your ideas to life.

Pushing the Boundaries of What's Possible with Glass

Glass is a versatile and compelling medium that invites artists to push the boundaries of what's possible. As you advance in your glass fusing journey, consider how you can break the conventional rules of the craft. This might involve experimenting with unconventional shapes, combining glass with other materials like metal or wood, or creating large-scale installations that challenge traditional perceptions of glass art. By pushing these boundaries, you can develop a distinctive style that sets your work apart. Innovation often comes from questioning the status quo, and in doing so, you may discover new possibilities that redefine what can be achieved in glass fusing.

Making a Lasting Impact with Your Art

Ultimately, the goal of any artist is to make a lasting impact with their work. Whether you aspire to create pieces that resonate on a personal level, contribute to the broader art community, or even make a statement in public spaces, your glass art has the potential to leave a lasting impression. Consider how your work can tell a story, evoke emotions, or inspire others. As you continue to refine your craft and develop your unique voice as an artist, you'll find that your creations not only reflect your journey but also influence the world around you. Glass fusing offers a powerful medium for making art that is both beautiful and meaningful, with the potential to impact viewers in profound ways.

APPENDICES

Glossary of Glass Fusing Terms

Understanding the language and terminology used in glass fusing is essential for anyone delving into this craft. The following glossary provides definitions of commonly used terms, helping to demystify the technical jargon and industry language you'll encounter as you advance in your glass fusing journey.

- Annealing: The process of slowly cooling fused glass to relieve internal stresses. Proper annealing is crucial to ensure the durability and stability of the finished piece.
- COE (Coefficient of Expansion): A measure of how much a material expands when heated and contracts when cooled. In glass fusing, it's vital to use glass with the same COE to prevent cracking or breaking during the fusing process.
- Dichroic Glass: A type of glass that displays two different colors depending on the angle of light and the background color. It's often used to add sparkle and dimension to fused glass projects.
- Firing Schedule: A set of instructions that outline the temperature changes in the kiln during the fusing process. It includes ramp rates (how quickly the temperature rises), soak times (how long the temperature is held steady), and cooling rates.
- Frit: Small pieces of crushed glass used in fusing to create designs, add texture, or fill in gaps between larger pieces of glass.
- Kiln Wash: A protective coating applied to kiln shelves and molds to prevent fused glass from sticking during firing.

- Slumping: A technique in glass fusing where the glass is heated until it softens and takes the shape of a mold. Slumping is often used to create bowls, plates, and other shaped items.
- Tack Fusing: A method of fusing glass pieces together at a lower temperature, resulting in a textured surface where the individual pieces are still slightly raised.
- Thermal Shock: The stress and potential cracking that occurs when glass is exposed to sudden temperature changes. Proper temperature control during firing and cooling helps prevent thermal shock.
- Vent Hole: A small opening in the kiln that allows air to escape, preventing bubbles and uneven heating during the firing process.

Understanding these terms will not only help you communicate more effectively within the glass fusing community but will also deepen your understanding of the processes and techniques involved in this intricate art form.

Firing Schedules and Temperature Charts

Firing schedules are critical to the success of any glass fusing project. Each type of glass and project requires a specific firing schedule to achieve the desired results. Below, you'll find detailed firing schedules for different types of glass and projects, along with quick reference charts for kiln temperatures and times.

Detailed Firing Schedules for Different Types of Glass and Projects

1. Standard Full Fusing Schedule

- Ramp 1: 300°F per hour to 1000°F, hold for 10 minutes

- Ramp 2: 600°F per hour to 1450°F, hold for 10 minutes
- Ramp 3: Full speed to 950°F, hold for 60 minutes (annealing)
- Ramp 4: 100°F per hour to 700°F, then off

2. Tack Fusing Schedule

- Ramp 1: 200°F per hour to 1100°F, hold for 10 minutes
- Ramp 2: 500°F per hour to 1350°F, hold for 5 minutes
- Ramp 3: Full speed to 950°F, hold for 60 minutes (annealing)
- Ramp 4: 100°F per hour to 700°F, then off

3. Slumping Schedule

- Ramp 1: 150°F per hour to 1150°F, hold for 10 minutes
- Ramp 2: 300°F per hour to 1250°F, hold for 10 minutes
- Ramp 3: Full speed to 950°F, hold for 60 minutes (annealing)
- Ramp 4: 100°F per hour to 700°F, then off

4. Kiln Casting Schedule

- Ramp 1: 200°F per hour to 1200°F, hold for 30 minutes
- Ramp 2: 400°F per hour to 1600°F, hold for 60 minutes
- Ramp 3: Full speed to 950°F, hold for 90 minutes (annealing)
- Ramp 4: 100°F per hour to 700°F, then off

Quick Reference Charts for Kiln Temperatures and Times

These charts provide a quick reference for the most common temperatures and times used in glass fusing, helping you to quickly set up your kiln for different projects.

Process	Temperature Range	Hold Time	Notes
Full Fusing	1450°F - 1500°F	10-15 min	For fully melting and fusing glass layers
Tack Fusing	1300°F - 1350°F	5-10 min	For partially fusing glass layers
Slumping	1200°F - 1300°F	10-20 min	For shaping glass into molds
Fire Polishing	1350°F - 1400°F	5-10 min	For achieving a smooth, glossy surface
Annealing	900°F - 950°F	60-90 min	Essential for relieving stress in the glass

Process   Temperature Range Hold Time   Notes

Full Fusing 1450°F - 1500°F 10-15 min For fully melting and fusing glass layers

Tack Fusing 1300°F - 1350°F 5-10 min For partially fusing glass layers

Slumping 1200°F - 1300°F 10-20 min For shaping glass into molds

Fire Polishing 1350°F - 1400°F 5-10 min For achieving a smooth, glossy surface

Annealing 900°F - 950°F 60-90 min Essential for relieving stress in the glass

Having these firing schedules and temperature charts at your fingertips will help you achieve consistent and successful results in your glass fusing projects.

Troubleshooting Guide

Even with careful planning and execution, issues can arise during the glass fusing process. This troubleshooting guide provides quick solutions for common problems, tips for avoiding issues in the first place, and advice on when to seek help from experts.

Quick Solutions for Common Problems

1. Bubbles in Fused Glass

- Cause: Trapped air between layers of glass or in the kiln.
- Solution: Use thinner layers of glass, ensure the glass is clean and free of debris, and adjust your firing schedule to allow more time for air to escape.

2. Cracked Glass

- Cause: Thermal shock or improper annealing.
- Solution: Ensure gradual temperature changes during firing and cooling, and follow a proper annealing schedule.

3. Devitrification

- Cause: Glass surface crystallizes, resulting in a cloudy or rough texture.
- Solution: Clean glass thoroughly before fusing, avoid over-firing, and use a devitrification spray if necessary.

4. Uneven Slumping

- Cause: Uneven heating or improper mold preparation.
- Solution: Ensure the mold is properly coated with kiln wash, and adjust your firing schedule to allow for more uniform heating.

Tips for Avoiding Issues in the First Place

- Proper Glass Preparation: Always clean your glass thoroughly before fusing to remove any oils, dust, or contaminants that could affect the outcome.
- Accurate Firing Schedules: Follow the recommended firing schedules for the type of glass and project you are working on. Adjust based on your kiln's behavior.
- Kiln Maintenance: Regularly inspect and maintain your kiln, including checking for damaged elements, replacing kiln wash, and ensuring the kiln is level.

When to Seek Help: Consulting with Experts

If you encounter persistent issues or are unsure about a particular aspect of glass fusing, don't hesitate to seek help from more experienced glass artists or kiln technicians.

Online forums, local art communities, and workshops are great resources for finding expert advice and solutions to complex problems.

Resources and Further Reading

Continuing your education in glass fusing is essential to advancing your skills and expanding your creative horizons. The following resources provide valuable information, inspiration, and opportunities to connect with other glass artists.

Recommended Books and Articles on Glass Fusing

- "Contemporary Fused Glass" by Brad Walker: A comprehensive guide covering advanced techniques and artistic approaches in glass fusing.
- "Introduction to Glass Fusing" by Petra Kaiser: An excellent resource for beginners, offering step-by-step instructions and project ideas.
- "Fused Glass Handbook" by Graham Stone: A detailed exploration of the technical aspects of glass fusing, including firing schedules and troubleshooting tips.

Websites, Blogs, and Online Communities for Glass Artists

- Warm Glass: A leading online resource for glass fusing enthusiasts, featuring tutorials, firing schedules, and a vibrant community forum.
- Glass Campus: An educational website offering free tutorials, videos, and articles on various glass art techniques.
- FusedGlass.org: A site dedicated to all things glass fusing, including project ideas, product reviews, and a community gallery.

List of Glass Art Museums and Exhibitions Worldwide

- The Corning Museum of Glass (Corning, NY, USA): Home to one of the world's most comprehensive collections of glass art, including fused glass.
- The Toledo Museum of Art Glass Pavilion (Toledo, OH, USA): A dedicated space for glass art, featuring exhibitions and live glassblowing demonstrations.
- Victoria and Albert Museum (London, UK): Hosts a significant collection of historical and contemporary glass art, including works by renowned glass artists.
- Musée du Verre (Conches-en-Ouche, France): Focused on modern glass art, this museum showcases contemporary works, including innovative glass fusing pieces, offering inspiration and insight into the evolving craft.
- Glass Art Society Annual Conference: An international event that brings together glass artists from around the world. The conference includes exhibitions, lectures, and workshops, providing a platform for learning and networking.
- Ebeltoft Glass Museum (Ebeltoft, Denmark): This museum specializes in contemporary glass art, offering exhibitions that highlight the latest trends and techniques in glass fusing and other glassworking methods.
- Pilchuck Glass School (Stanwood, WA, USA): While not a museum, this renowned institution offers immersive workshops and courses in glass art, including fusing. It's a great place to refine your skills and meet other passionate glass artists.

These resources, books, websites, and institutions provide a wealth of knowledge and inspiration for glass fusing enthusiasts. Whether you're a beginner or an experienced artist, they offer valuable insights into techniques, materials, and the artistic possibilities of fused glass.

Printed in Great Britain
by Amazon